An Inspirational Guide through Troubled Times

JEREMIAH

a Devotional Commentary

Tom Birch

Print ISBN: 978-1-4866-1940-5
eBook ISBN: 978-1-4866-1941-2

Word Alive Press
119 De Baets Street, Winnipeg, MB R2J 3R9
www.wordalivepress.ca

WORD ALIVE
—PRESS—

Cataloguing in Publication may be obtained through Library and Archives Canada

What people are saying

In this accessible and readable account of the prophet Jeremiah, Tom Birch provides the reader with a solid foundation on the prophet's life and writings. Written in a succinct fashion, this devotional commentary skilfully applies the principles found in Jeremiah to our contemporary lives. I enthusiastically recommend this book to any reader for the insights it provides on a difficult portion of scripture, as well as for its devotional enrichment.

—Danny Legault
Senior Pastor of Westside Family Fellowship
Prince George, BC

Tom's masterful treatment of Jeremiah offers detailed historical, theological, and practical material that will challenge mature believers to deepen their faith in God, and older generations to empower newer generations. As you read through and reflect on *Jeremiah: An Inspirational Guide through Troubled Times*, you're bound to experience true peace and contentment with God. I commend this work.

—Dr. Roger Helland, DMin
District Minister, Baptist General Conference Alberta
Author of *The Devout Life*, *Magnificent Surrender*
and *Missional Spirituality*

My life has been a wonderful journey with God, which has been spurred on by the awesome wife He gave me. She has convinced me that I can do almost anything, but she also reminds me that only those things done for Christ have any value. I dedicate this, my first book, to Evelyn, who has stood by me for more than thirty-six years.

He lifted me out of the slimy pit,
out of the mud and mire;
he set my feet on a rock
and gave me a firm place to stand.
—Psalm 40:2

God's extravagant mercy is offered to a nation who has rejected Him. As they look for meaning in money, power, sex, and false spirituality, God sends His prophet to point the way to true peace and contentment with God.

CONTENTS

INTRODUCTION

Doom, death, destruction, and judgement! Why would anyone read, let alone write, a book on the life of Jeremiah? Nicknamed "the weeping prophet" for good reason, Jeremiah lived during one of the greatest persecutions in the history of the Jewish people. By God's decree, Jeremiah saw the destroyer, King Nebuchadnezzar of Babylon, kill over 90 per cent of the population and raze both the temple and the holy city of Jerusalem to the ground. Those who weren't killed were sent into exile to Babylon. No other devastation came close to this until the Second World War when the global centre of Jewish life, which was in Poland, was eradicated. Who would want to re-live such terrible times?

Christians see the story of God's redemption throughout the Bible as our story. Seth, Enoch, and Noah are featured before the flood, followed by Shem, Abraham, Moses, and the Jewish people after the flood. In the New Testament, Christ fulfills God's promised salvation. The Gentile church is the wild branch grafted into the vine of God's people. The story of Jeremiah isn't just history for the Jewish people, but it's our story as well. It's a story for everyone, because God is the God of all people, and Jeremiah was specifically sent as "*a prophet to the nations*" (Jeremiah 1:5b).

What will we find in Jeremiah, other than death and judgement? The answer is love, mercy, forgiveness, and grace (2 Chronicles 36:15). The Bible displays these attributes of God along with His justice, and they shine brightest when justice demands judgement. Forgiveness isn't required where there is no transgression: "*It is not the healthy who need a doctor, but the sick*" (Mark 2:17).

Our culture parallels Jeremiah's. People seek spirituality but not God. "Hooking up" is considered normal and expected. Infidelity is rampant, as is abortion. The poor are exploited rather than provided for. Our legal system is used to pervert justice. These same things were condemned in Jeremiah's time (Ezekiel 18:1–32). Because Jeremiah's story occurs at a time much like our own, we too need to know that the hand of God is outstretched toward us in love.

Like the people of Judah during most of Jeremiah's life, we're not yet at the point of judgement; rather, "*God again set a certain day, calling it 'Today.' ... 'Today, if you hear his voice, do not harden your hearts*'" (Hebrews 4:7). Although the author of Hebrews uses the word "today," the meaning in this context is better translated as "now," as in "*now is the day of salvation*" (2 Corinthians 6:2b). We are living in the "now" of God, and in this story, we can hear the voice of God calling in love. So why would anyone want to read the story of Jeremiah? To rekindle hope.

This retelling of the life of Jeremiah is a devotional commentary. It reads gently between the lines to chronologically connect the biblical vignettes of the life of the prophet. It peers into the hearts and motivations of the characters, based on their actions. From there, it speaks to our hearts today. May it bring you hope for our generation as it has for me!

Chapter One

BORN FOR TROUBLED TIMES

O ur story does not begin when we are born. Rather, it begins with the setting that we are born into—a time, place, and family that we don't choose, with a destiny we must grow to understand. So it was for Jeremiah, a boy born to a Levitical family. The conflicts that would shape his ministry had been developing for centuries. He wasn't particularly remarkable, nor was the small town of Anathoth, where he came into the world. But his destiny would terrify kings and reshape nations for generations. Indeed, his life can still impact us today.

We live in an individualistic time when we can feel disassociated from our history. Some people have been born into harsh circumstances and may wish that they could disconnect completely from their families. But God has placed us into the tapestry of history exactly where we are for a purpose. The more we understand the influences that have shaped us, the better positioned we'll be to give our lives to God and see where He takes us.

Jeremiah's world had also been shaped by major events reaching back hundreds of years. Born in 650 B.C., Jeremiah went unnoticed for many years. His father named him and only expected that he would grow up to be a priest. But to comprehend his destiny, we must go back more than three hundred years and understand his beginnings.

Hundreds of years before Jeremiah's birth, the nation of Israel had expanded to the greatest height of its power under King Solomon. But as he was coming to the end of his life, he said, *"I hated all the things I had toiled for under the sun, because I must leave them to the one who comes after me. And who knows whether that person will be wise or foolish?"* (Ecclesiastes 2:18–19a). He expressed a general concern about heirs, but I think Solomon also knew that his son was of the "foolish" variety.

During his rule, Solomon had been a firm king. He was the wisest man who ever lived, so he never doubted that what he was doing was the best course of action and that it would achieve the greatest good for the nation. However, his ways had seemed harsh to some individuals, and the taxes he collected for the common good had been very high. When he died, the people's discontent was about to boil over.

When Solomon's son Rehoboam took the throne, some of the people asked if he would lower the taxes. His father's advisors encouraged him to do this, saying that it would win the love of the people. However, his friends, whom he had brought on as new advisors, suggested that it would be a sign of weakness. They said that if he gave in, the people would never respect him. They even wrote the most disastrous political speech in the Bible by telling him to say to the people, *"My little finger is thicker than my father's waist. My father laid on you a heavy yoke; I will make it even heavier"* (1 Kings 12:10b-11a). Alas, Rehoboam decided to go with the advice of his friends. When he refused to give the common people any relief, a tax revolt split the nation.

One of Solomon's previous officials was a man named Jeroboam. A prophet had told him that when Solomon died, he would become king of the ten northern Hebrew states. He didn't know if this prophecy would come true or not, but he did position himself to take control if the moment came. During the tax revolt, ten of the twelve states of Israel followed Jeroboam and made him their king, leaving only Judah and Benjamin in the Southern Kingdom. Benjamin would have followed Jeroboam too, except the state of Judah was shaped like a doughnut, with Benjamin as the hole in the centre. Their fate was bound together with Judah's. When Jeroboam took over the Northern Nation, it kept the name of Israel. The Southern Nation took the name of Judah, after the larger of the two states that comprised it.

This map shows the Northern Kingdom of Israel and the Southern Kingdom of Judah. In the Bible, the term "Israelites" can refer to all the Hebrew people prior to the split in the kingdom, or to just the people in the Northern Kingdom after the split. Also, it can be used to refer to both the Judeans and the Israelites when speaking of the chosen people of God as a whole. This can make it a confusing term. Therefore, except when quoting scriptures, this book refers to the two states as the Northern Kingdom (or nation) and Judah (or the Southern Kingdom). The people as a whole are referred to as either Jewish or Hebrews.

This was a tenuous situation, exacerbated by the fact that all the major festivals for the Hebrew people were celebrated at the temple in Jerusalem, which was the capital of Judah. Jeroboam feared that if he allowed his country to maintain the heart of their faith in Jerusalem, they would eventually want political reunification. If that happened in his lifetime, he would be executed for treason (1 Kings 12:27).

Jeroboam decided to give the Northern Kingdom of Israel its own places for worship. He had altars built in the cities of Dan and Bethel. He also had an idol, shaped like a golden calf, cast for each city, telling the people, "*It is too much for you to go ... to Jerusalem. Here are your gods, Israel, who brought you up out of Egypt*" (1 Kings 12:28b). Now they could celebrate nearer to home and not be reliant on the temple, which was under the control of Solomon's son in the south.

Jeroboam hadn't intended to start a new religion, just a politically expedient parallel expression of the faith. To do this, however, he had to ignore what Moses had instructed about where the temple should be located. Jerusalem was that place, and Jeroboam knew it. The Hebrew people had struggled on and off with their faithfulness to Yahweh[1] ever since they'd entered the land, and now those in the Northern Nation had a faith that was based on the scriptures being selectively optional. They took full advantage of it.

They quickly adopted the evil practises of the nations around them. They worshipped gods that led them into sexual orgies, and they normalized incest, child abuse, and prostitution. This led to unwanted children, so they worshipped Moloch and burned the infants alive, all the while feeling self-righteous. They took advantage of the poor and became violent. They practised divination and quickly left behind their faith in the true God.

If we think that we can press the Bible into our cultural mould instead of submitting to it and allowing it to reshape us, then we've fallen into Jeroboam's error. Our culture has abandoned biblical morals and embraced sexually indulgent lifestyles. We celebrate the right to abortion the way child sacrifice to Moloch was celebrated. We take

---

1   Yahweh is the name of God, which means "I am." In many Bible versions, it is written as "Lord" with small capitals.

advantage of the poor, or just ignore their needs. Our culture desperately needs God's mercy to pull us out of the pit we've fallen into. For that to happen, the church must stand firm on the scriptures, embracing the whole message of God. If we decide that parts of the Bible can be ignored because they offend our cultural beliefs, then God's entire message becomes optional. We become God's judge, censuring Him in case He says something wrong. That was the legacy of Jeroboam. We must not let it be the church's legacy to the next generation.

When we live in fear of people instead of God, we try to please people and end up not pleasing God. Jeroboam was afraid to allow his people to go to the temple. As a result, he set them on a path away from God. In doing so, he thought himself worldly-wise, but he planted the seeds of destruction in his nation.

Within 250 years, God allowed Assyria to conquer the Northern Kingdom of Israel as punishment for their sins. As was common practice at that time, the conquering nation deported most of the people so that they would be absorbed into the greater imperial culture. Assyria also brought deportees from other conquered lands to intermingle with the poorer Hebrews left behind. Within a generation after the conquest, the northern people were a mixed race with even more eclectic and evil religious practises.

———※———

During this time, the Southern Kingdom of Judah continued, sometimes following God and sometimes looking more like their northern counterpart. Then around 700 B.C., a few decades after the conquest of the Northern Kingdom by the Assyrians, Manasseh came to the throne in Judah. Jeremiah was born during his reign. Manasseh would reign for fifty-five years and earn himself the distinction of being the wickedest king that ever sat on the throne in Judah.

Manasseh knew that the northern land was now part of the Assyrian Empire, but he also knew that the people who lived there were still part of the Hebrew people, diluted as their bloodline was with those who had been brought to live there from other nations. His actions showed that he wanted to finally re-unify the people, so he carefully began to woo them to join their Judean kin in worship at the temple in Jerusalem.

How do you bring together a people whose religion is so different than yours? Manasseh's father, Hezekiah, had been a good king, and under him the people had been dedicated to Yahweh. The Northern Kingdom was anything but. They had many gods, and Yahweh was only one option. It's one thing to hold an inter-faith meeting where we affirm that we can love and respect each other despite our different perspectives on God, but to integrate beliefs and practices that are in direct opposition to the truth of scripture means that you must leave the truth behind. This is what Manasseh did. He presumed that unity was a greater good than truth and righteousness, so he welcomed the northern Jews along with all their evil practises. Over the years of his reign, the pure faith of Hezekiah was lost in the worship of detestable idols.

The true believers didn't go down without a fight, and Manasseh filled Jerusalem from end to end with the blood of the innocent (2 Kings 21:16). As priests and prophets would call him out and remind him of the Law, he would have them killed. Then, to deal more directly with the problem, he had the Law banned altogether. We're never directly told that Manasseh banned any parts of the Law; however, we know that the Law of Moses was well known to Manasseh's father, but his grandson, Josiah, had never heard of it (and Josiah's father only reigned for two years). Clearly Manasseh had removed the standard of truth.

We can imagine that the Law posed a problem for Manasseh. Perhaps he labelled it "hate speech," as some do today. The Law insisted that the northern practices had to stop before the people could come together, which stood in the way of re-unification and seemed harsh and discriminatory. So Manasseh outlawed it and destroyed every copy he could find. With the Law destroyed, and the righteous who remembered it dead, Manasseh was free to corrupt his people as he saw fit. And corrupt them he did. He led the way in worship to gods that encouraged the people to practise witchcraft and divination, abuse the poor in pursuit of wealth and power, commit incest, prostitute their own daughters, and sacrifice the unwanted children that were born out of their sins. Manasseh rebuilt the high places that his father had torn down. He erected altars to Baal, put an Asherah pole in the temple along with altars to the stars and planets, sacrificed his own children, practised divination and sought omens, consulted mediums, and murdered anyone who got in his way.

In the last decade of Manasseh's life, Jeremiah was born. A time when anything was acceptable except the truth. A time when everything could be tolerated except righteousness. A time of sexual abandon and dysfunctional families. A scripture-less time when everyone did what was right in their own eyes. It could have been our time.

A few years after Jeremiah was born, King Manasseh was captured. Perhaps some of Jeremiah's earliest memories involved hearing that the king had been taken by the Assyrians to prison in Babylon.[2] This would have happened when Jeremiah was barely a toddler. The Assyrians were undoubtedly concerned about their hold on the northern lands of Israel and had noticed Manasseh's attempts to woo the people to Judah. At this time, the Assyrians may not have wanted to expend the resources required to deploy an army to take over Judah; however, they could capture and humble the king, teaching him to be a faithful ally and not meddle in lands belonging to their empire.

While the king was held captive, Manasseh's son, Amon, managed the kingdom and carried on where his father had left off. God, however, was working in Manasseh's heart, reminding him about the Law he had known as a child and the evil he had done to suppress it. We know nothing of his time in prison except that it was in that Babylonian dungeon that Manasseh repented. Shortly after he did, God released him to return to Jerusalem (2 Chronicles 33:12–13).

God's miracles, such as the parting of the Red Sea, are amazing. But often He works through the natural order and accomplishes just as much with miraculous timing and divine providence. The Assyrians had conquered Babylon a few generations earlier, but they hadn't

---

2   During their rise to power, the Assyrians had taken over most of the Babylonian lands and still held the city of Babylon.

completely destroyed the Babylonians. It would be another fifteen or twenty years before the Babylonians reclaimed their capital city, but for now the descendants of that conquered race were testing their strength. The Assyrians decided they had more important issues than keeping Manasseh locked up. Shortly after he had been brought to Babylon, the Assyrians found themselves too busy with the resurgence of the Babylonians to continue to hold Manasseh, so they contented themselves with the hope that they had made their point, and they let him go. This was how God fulfilled His plan for Manasseh.

Manasseh returned to Judah full of hope that he could use the last days of his life to set things right and undo the evil he had done. He now had two passions for how he wanted to be remembered. He still desired to re-unify all the Jewish people, but now the plan was to do so in obedience to Yahweh. Manasseh serves as an example of how God's mercy and grace are always offered to all people. After fifty years of rule, in which God proclaimed him to be the evilest, most murderous king in the history of Judah, His love sent him to jail as a divine time-out to consider his path. When Manasseh repented, God accepted him. There is no depth of depravity from which God cannot draw us back, and there is no age at which it's too late for us to turn to Him. We may have spent our entire life opposed to God and righteousness, but if we respond to His Spirit in faith and repentance, He will instantly accept us into His family and forgive all our sins.

There are, however, consequences to our choices that may not be reversible. Not only had Manasseh worshipped false gods, but he had taught his son and the people of Judah to do so as well. God declared that because of Manasseh's sin, Judah would be conquered and exiled just like the Northern Kingdom had been. The soul of the nation had fallen with Manasseh, and even though he was redeemed, the rest of the people were not.

Manasseh still hoped for some fruit from his repentance. He came back to Jerusalem ready to reform the nation. What he found was that his son, who had been acting king for a year or more, was not prepared to see everything change. Manasseh did achieve some minor reforms, but nothing of any consequence. Likely his officials, and even his son, were humouring him, but behind his back they made sure that the social order wasn't significantly disrupted. When he died a few years later, things were just as bad, or worse, under Amon as they had been under Manasseh. God had not saved Manasseh to use him to undo the evil he had done; God had saved Manasseh because he loved him and wanted to save him. We may think that we're not important enough or good enough for God to love, but that's foolish. When we study Manasseh, we see that, thankfully, we don't need to be important, good, or even useful in order to be loved by God.

God also had mercy on Manasseh and granted him some consolation before he died. His son no longer needed his father's help to run the kingdom, so when Manasseh returned, he spent a great deal of time with his grandson, Josiah. Josiah was six when his grandfather died, but Manasseh's repentance impacted him deeply. For Manasseh to have touched Josiah as he did, he must have had time to play with his grandson and watch the boy respond with innocence to his grandfather's sorrow over what he had done. I'm sure that Manasseh didn't think much would come of it, but he planted a seed in Josiah's young heart, which in time would grow into something beautiful.

If any Old Testament story portrays God's mercy, it's the story of Manasseh, a man who spent his whole life in fierce opposition to God. Then, at the very end of his life, he repented and was forgiven. More than that, he was given a few years to play with his grandson and change a life. He may have wanted to change the lives of millions, but it was enough that God allowed him to change one. And he didn't do it by enacting great laws but with hugs and children's games. What greater testament can there be to God's love for us while we are still sinners

Chapter Two

THE AWAKENING

The evil King Manasseh died when Jeremiah was a youth of about ten. By this time, he was training to be a priest in the corrupt priesthood in Anathoth. Even so, Jeremiah grew up dedicated to the God of his fathers and not the gods of the king. We know very little about his parentage beyond the fact that he was from a Levitical family and was true to Yahweh. That alone tells us that his parents were true believers who taught him what they remembered about the Law of Moses, which by then was lost. Unfortunately, we know nothing else about his early life until fifteen years later when he began his ministry; however, we do know what was happening in the kingdom at large as he was growing up.

When Manasseh died, his son, Amon, took the throne at the young age of twenty-two. God's decree for him was that he "*increased his guilt*" (2 Chronicles 33:23). His own officials conspired against him, and he was assassinated at the palace. His son, Josiah, was made king in his place. The boy, who two years earlier had been playing with his repentant grandfather, was now the king of Judah at the age of only eight.

Josiah had inherited his grandfather's desires to serve God and to re-unify the Northern Kingdom with Judah; however, he was only a boy. His advisors likely managed the day-to-day running of the country for the first few years while he spent his time learning how to be a king. By the time he was sixteen, "*he began to seek the God of his father David*" (2 Chronicles 34:3). This must have been a hard task without the Law of Moses and with priests who were more indoctrinated in the ways of the false Baals and animistic gods than they were in the path of the true creator. God said of the Judean Hebrews that they had as many gods as they had towns (Jeremiah 2:28). Nonetheless, Josiah sought God in prayer and likely looked for anyone who had remained faithful and could instruct him. There would have been a lot of skepticism, though. People may have wondered if this wasn't just a trap to lure in the last remaining true believers, since pagan worship was still in full force at this time.

Slowly over the next four years, and probably against the advice of his court, Josiah decided that if he was serious, he needed to purge the land of false worship. By the time Josiah was twenty years old, God led him to begin a purge in Jerusalem and Judah. He started to get rid of the high places along with the Asherah poles and idols located there. Typically, the highest point in every town would have a shrine to the fertility goddess. Here the girls (and sometimes boys) were forced to be priestesses (or priests) in the cult. The men would go up to the shrine and give their "donation." Then they would enter and "worship" through prostitution with these servants of the goddess, many of whom were young children.

We think of prostitution as part of organized crime; we don't relate it to religious worship, except in some rare cases of obscure cults. A generation ago, our culture began to legitimize prostitution, pornography, and many previously unaccepted sexual behaviours through *Playboy* magazine and all the spin-offs that followed it. But in the ancient world, prostitution was legitimized through religion, and the pimps were called high priests. We lack an awareness of ancient cultural practices, so we don't always understand why such drastic measures were taken by righteous kings and prophets to remove this kind of worship. It wasn't bigotry against other faiths but a crackdown on crime that impacted the most vulnerable members of society.

Today, young men are raised on pornography. TV is full of suggestive scenes and nudity that weren't acceptable a few decades ago. Our culture has followed the evil path that Alfred Kinsey and Hugh Hefner laid out for us, and even in the church we're desensitized to this unrighteousness. As things were changing in the 1960s and 1970s, the church was taken completely off-guard. Our youth were bombarded with the idea that it was limiting and wrong to reserve sex for the marriage bed in a committed, lifelong union between one man and one woman. Church leadership was too embarrassed to preach about what was being taught in our culture, and the older members of our congregations were too embarrassed to hear about it. We ignored it and hoped it would be self-evident that it was wrong. As a result, surveys now show that 68 per cent of church-going men view pornography on a regular basis, and 33 per cent of women aged thirteen to twenty-four are caught in the same trap.[3] It's thought at worst to be a victimless crime and at best a normal and expected part of life. But the men and women who create it are victims; our families and relationships are victims; our own souls are victims. Pornography scrambles our moral compass and opens us up to all other aspects of the sex trade and our hook-up culture. This leaves a trail of abused women, broken relationships, and unwanted pregnancies, just like in Josiah's time.

In the second half of the last century, men led our culture down this path. Today, God is calling the men of our churches to lead His people back out. Praise God for the current movement to tear down the high places! God's mercy and forgiveness are vast, and He offers them to us freely. We're fighting the same sexually addictive behaviours that Josiah fought, and out of His love for us, God is giving the church a voice to speak to this stronghold in our culture. Groups like Pure Desire, Kingdom Works, Conquer Series, and many others are boldly tearing these high places out of one life at a time.

Without the Law, Josiah may not have known what was right, but he knew this was wrong, so he began to purge it from the country. God hadn't shown Josiah much yet, but He had given him some understanding. Then He let Josiah demonstrate his allegiance by his first faltering steps of obedience.

God doesn't often show us the end when we're only at the beginning; rather, He shows us the first step and asks us to take it. Many

---

3   Luke Gibbons, "Church's Dirty Little Secret," *Conquer Series*, accessed October 5, 2019, https://conquerseries.com/set-free-stats/.

times as we take that step, we think the path is going to lead one way. As we walk down it and God reveals more, we need to refine our direction based on this later revelation of His purpose in our life. God is most concerned about our obedience and that we follow where He directs us. He will sort out the rest of the details if we're faithful in the first steps.

For Josiah, the next step of revelation was difficult. After Josiah's first year of shutting down child trafficking and prostitution in the high places, the prophet Jeremiah began his ministry. Josiah couldn't have been less pleased. One would hope that if God was to raise up a prophet during such a time of renewal, it would be a prophet who would commend the king for his passion for God and righteousness. For four years, Josiah had prayed and sought God. For another year, against the advice of many, he had been freeing sex slaves by shutting down the worship of the fertility goddess. Five years of faithfulness! And then Jeremiah was called and began to preach his unpopular message.

Back in Anathoth, Jeremiah had an encounter with God. We don't know if it was a dream or a waking vision, but God told him, *"Before I formed you in the womb I knew you, before you were born I set you apart; I appointed you as a prophet to the nations"* (Jeremiah 1:5). Like He did for Jeremiah, God has plans for all of us and is intimately involved in our lives from before our conception. We probably haven't been given a task as prominent as Jeremiah's, but we are created to do the good works God planned for us before our conception (Ephesians 2:10).

Often we make excuses, because we don't think we're capable, or perhaps we don't feel holy or worthy enough to be used by God. Maybe we're afraid of doing what we believe He's asking of us. God will take care of our inabilities as we step out in obedience. It may be a longer process than we'd like. It may mean having to deal with sin in our lives, or going to school to learn new skills, but God will develop what He wants in us if we're faithful to begin.

Jeremiah complained that he was too young (Jeremiah 1:6), but God was firm with him too. The prophet would have to go to whomever he was sent and speak the words that God would tell him to speak (Jeremiah 1:7). God told him that he would bring messages that would uproot, tear down, destroy, and overthrow nations. But he would also build and plant (Jeremiah 1:10). It would be a long time before the building and planting came to be, but he was given hope that his messages would not only be negative. In obedience, he moved to Jerusalem and began his ministry.

Jeremiah's ministry upset the king, however. What did he preach about that was so disconcerting? Well, he started with a vision of a boiling pot of God's wrath pouring over Judea from the north (Jeremiah 1:13–16). He explained that a recent drought wasn't just a chance happening but had been sent by God to show the people that their idols could not bring rain (Jeremiah 14:22). He railed against the people, saying that none were righteous (Jeremiah 5:1–31). Through it all ran the foundational prediction that the utter and complete destruction of Jerusalem and the temple was coming, along with the exile of all the people who survived. Jeremiah continued this preaching for the next five years.

To make matters worse, God commanded Jeremiah not to marry, because he wouldn't be able to save his wife or children when the disaster came. Nor was he to celebrate with those who did marry (Jeremiah 16:1–4). He was also forbidden from going to funerals or comforting those who had lost loved ones (Jeremiah 16:5). As a prophet, his life was to be just as much of a message as his prophecies, so every time he refused a wedding invitation or shunned a funeral, he explained that it was because in the coming judgement, the living would envy the dead (Jeremiah 8:3). Talk about a kill-joy to be around! Jeremiah must have wished that just once he could give one of those "building and planting" messages. He must have watched Josiah and his reforms and longed to be able to commend the king and predict peace and re-unification for the Jewish people.

One of the first conflicts with the king may have arisen over Jeremiah's pronouncement on the droughts they were having. Droughts in the ancient world meant that people starved to death. Today, food transportation networks allow us to move vast quantities of food around the world, so it takes a large and sustained drought, and usually some political corruption, to impact people with anything worse than high food prices. But those networks weren't in place in biblical times, nor could most foods be preserved as they are now. Because of this, even a small local drought could mean death to the people living in the immediate area. They took these things very seriously and would look for reasons why they were happening.

The people would have looked to what Josiah had been doing for the cause of the drought. He had stopped the rituals to the fertility goddess, and now they were experiencing famines. While the people were pressuring the king on this front, Jeremiah was preaching that the lack of rain was caused by the lack of repentance in Judah. Jeremiah said that he was pleading with God to help the people despite their sins (Jeremiah 14:7–9). But God countered that their false prophets were leading them astray, and that if they didn't change, there would be nothing but death for the country.

On the one side, the people accused Josiah of causing the problem with his reforms, but from the other side, Jeremiah told him that his reform hadn't even penetrated the surface of the problem. For the king, that must have felt like an unfair slap in the face. Where was God's approval for all the good he was doing? Surely Jeremiah couldn't be a true prophet if he couldn't see that the king should be supported and not attacked.

Taking a first step of obedience doesn't guarantee that we'll be commended. Sometimes, God still needs to teach us more. When He sees that we're open, then the real lessons can begin. We must not give up just because the road is more difficult than we'd hoped. If we persist, we'll see God's blessings on our faithfulness (Galatians 6:9). Josiah wouldn't see the big picture for a few more years, but it would come.

At one point, God told Jeremiah to buy a clay jar. He took it and any of the elders of Jerusalem who would go with him to the Valley of Ben Hinnom. This was the place just outside of Jerusalem where the inconvenient children—born of the people's incest, prostitution, and adultery—were sacrificed. When they got there, Jeremiah decreed judgement on the place, because the people had filled it with the blood of the innocent. He told the elders that God had renamed it the Valley of Slaughter, because God was going to slaughter the people there. He told them that a siege was coming on Jerusalem that would be so severe, the people would eat their own children and each other in order to survive. If they refused to repent for killing the children that He had given them, God was going to take back from them even the ones they wanted. Then, with a dramatic flare, Jeremiah smashed the jar he had carried and decreed that Jerusalem would likewise be smashed (Jeremiah 19:1–15).

Our culture has also embraced sexual promiscuity, but it doesn't cherish the children who are conceived as a result. We put our own lives first and discard our offspring by the hundreds of thousands. And we can't just blame individuals for their choices. This is a stronghold in our nations' beliefs. Every man who looks at pornography or participates in the hook-up culture is just as involved in the deaths of the aborted children as those who make the final decisions, whether or not they've fathered any of these precious lives. The God who gave us children as His blessing will not stand by while this goes on.

In the midst of this message, Jeremiah told the people that God said, *"Reform your ways and your actions and I will let you live in this place"* (Jeremiah 7:3b). There is mercy, forgiveness, and healing if we confess our sins and repent. Jeremiah's message highlighted how God was reaching out to the people, wanting to forgive and restore life for them, but they rejected every attempt. Today we still live in the "now" of God's patience. His hand is reaching out, just as it was in Jeremiah's lifetime, eager to forgive and restore. No matter what we've done, God can resurrect our dead hearts. This message of mercy was given to people who had been sacrificing their unwanted children to an evil demon. It applies today just as much as it did then. Even if we've been directly involved in sexual sins, and even if we've aborted the children God has given us as a result, complete forgiveness and restoration are available if we repent.

We know that women aren't always willing participants in sexual encounters but may instead be victims. There is healing in the work of Christ for this too. All sins, those that we have committed as well as the violence done against us, are dealt with at the cross of Christ. God longs to restore our souls and can do so through the innocent children that result from sexual violence. There is nothing new in our times that God hasn't been reaching throughout history to restore.

Jeremiah's message was not well received. After he brought the message of God's love for the children, and the pending judgement if the people continued to sacrifice them, he was beaten and left in the stocks overnight (Jeremiah 20:1–2). For the people, admitting they were wrong and repenting was too high a price to pay for God's mercy. They thought of themselves as righteous and didn't want to believe that they were murderers. Likewise today, when prolife proponents hold out God's love and mercy, they're accused of being hateful and hurtful toward women. Before the good news can be applied, we must accept the bad news of our sins, which seems unthinkable to many people. Yet the message of God's forgiveness remains, to be applied first to the church and then to a broken world.

Josiah did nothing to stop the harsh treatment of Jeremiah, revealing that he hadn't yet come to understand that God was speaking to the king too. Jeremiah's conversation with God that night bounced between singing praises and wishing he had never been born (Jeremiah 20:7–18). Sometimes in the church we get the impression that it's a sin to be depressed, because it shows a lack of trust in God. But God isn't afraid of our emotions. He not only accompanies us in our joy, but He walks beside us in our depression, and He gives us songs in the darkest of nights.

—————

Although he didn't understand why Jeremiah had been sent, Josiah remained faithful to what he did know during five years of reform, even while listening to Jeremiah preach disaster. Then Josiah began some long-overdue renovations on the temple, demonstrating a spiritual principle. When we remove sin, or even non-productive behaviours from our lives, we need to fill the void with new, godly disciplines. Josiah tore down the high places and then rebuilt the temple of God.

Figuratively, we need to do the same. For example, if we remove an un-righteous TV show from our life, we need to fill that hour with something else, such as reading Christian books or volunteering time for a good cause. If we leave a void, we'll be drawn back to the same thing we gave up. God wants to clear spaces in our lives to make room for what He's calling us to do.

As Josiah's workers were refurbishing the various rooms, they found a copy of the Law of Moses that had been hidden and preserved in the days of Manasseh. They brought it and read it to Josiah, and he began to understand the great depth of the sins of the people and how his minor reform hadn't even begun to bring the people back to Yahweh. Josiah's righteous heart was broken. He humbled himself before God in prayer and fasting and tore his clothes as a sign of his grief (2 Kings 22:8–11; 2 Chronicles 34:14–19). Yet after five years of Jeremiah's preaching, the king didn't seek him out to see what God would reveal about the situation. Rather, Josiah went to the prophetess Huldah. She was a righteous woman, also in Jerusalem. She told him that God was indeed going to destroy the nation for the great sins they had committed under Manasseh and were still committing; however, the judgement would come after Josiah's death, because he had humbled himself (2 Kings 22:12–20; 2 Chronicles 34:20–28). In this way, she confirmed the messages that Jeremiah had been preaching for the past five years, and her confirmation finally opened the king's heart to the prophet.

We aren't given the details of how Jeremiah and Josiah became friends, but evidence exists that later in their lives they enjoyed a great friendship. Shortly after the finding of the Law, Josiah invited Jeremiah to the palace, where Jeremiah helped in the instruction and training of Josiah's children (Lamentations 3:22). By this time, Josiah had two sons, twelve and ten years old. The elder, Eliakim, would later be forced to change his name and be remembered as Jehoiakim. The younger was Jehoahaz. Soon Josiah would have a third, Mattaniah, who would come to be known as Zedekiah, the last king of Judah. Jeremiah would help to raise all three of them.

After five years of ministry, during which the message God had given Jeremiah had isolated him so that he was nearly friendless, he formed a powerful connection with the righteous king of Judah. God was faithful to give him a deep and enduring relationship. By that time, Jeremiah must have given up on ever having such a close friend, since he had been forbidden to get married or celebrate or grieve with others. God, however, never leaves us to carry more sorrow than we can bear. He is with us through it all, and He knows what we need in this life and will provide it. His life still wasn't easy, but Jeremiah now had a companion with whom to share his burdens.

Chapter Three

THE GLORY YEARS

The glory days of Judah started with the finding of the Law! The rest of Josiah's short reign was a time of blessings. It only lasted thirteen more years, but they were years of dedication to Yahweh. The king, who was now twenty-six years old, and the prophet, who was not much older, were speaking and working in harmony under God.

At this point, Josiah knew what the Law required, and he wanted to rid the land of the evil that had come with the worship of false gods. He needed to finish the renovations on the temple and then complete his purge, both in Judah and in the Northern Kingdom, which was still officially under Assyrian rule. Although God's judgement, pronounced by Jeremiah, had been confirmed by Huldah, Josiah knew that God could relent if the people repented. This had happened many times in their history, and Jeremiah included the call back to God and His mercy in all his messages of impending destruction. Josiah hoped that he'd be able to atone for the nation's sins and avert God's wrath.

As soon as Josiah read the Law, he renewed the covenant they'd been breaking. He called the elders, priests, prophets, and all the people of Judah together and had the Law read to them at the temple. First, Josiah pledged himself to obey the covenant. Then he had all the people pledge themselves to it as well (2 Kings 23:1–3; 2 Chronicles 34:29–32). Following that, he ordered all the items for the worship of foreign gods removed from the temple, along with the altars to the sun, moon, and stars. He got rid of the male prostitutes that served at a shrine set up inside the temple itself, and he had all the priests of these gods killed.

The purge moved from the temple to all of Judah, and he desecrated the altars used to sacrifice children so that they could no longer be killed on them. Some of the altars he destroyed dated back to the time of King Solomon and had been made by Solomon for his foreign wives (2 Kings 23:4–14; 2 Chronicles 34:33).

Then Josiah travelled out of Judah and went to Bethel and the surrounding areas in the occupied Northern Kingdom. He didn't go very far over his border, but it was a bold move into Assyrian lands. He wanted to let the Hebrews from the Northern Kingdom know that although they were welcome to come to the temple in Jerusalem, their gods were not. Josiah destroyed the altar that Jeroboam had set up in Bethel centuries before when the kingdom had split over taxes (2 Kings 23:15–20). When Jeroboam had consecrated the altar in Bethel, a prophet had pronounced that a king from Judah named Josiah would destroy it one day (1 Kings 13:2). Josiah fulfilled this prophecy. Once he had found and read the Law, Josiah was quick to do everything in it.

When he had gotten rid of the public worship of all but Yahweh, Josiah returned home and held the greatest celebration of the Passover that had ever been observed in the land (2 Kings 23:22; 2 Chronicles 35:1–19). God said of Josiah that:

> *Neither before nor after Josiah was there a king like him who turned to the Lord as he did—with all his heart and with all his soul and with all his strength, in accordance with all the Law of Moses.*
>
> —2 Kings 23:25

Based on the number of animals and cakes eaten at Josiah's Passover, there must have been several million people in Jerusalem for the event. They had come from both Judah and the Northern Kingdom. Some of those present would go on to be fearless followers of God. Daniel, Shadrach, Meshach, and Abednego may have been there as very young children, or else they were born shortly afterwards. They were of the royal family and would have been guests of the king. At that time, Ezekiel would have been one or two years old. He was not from the royal family, but he was likely living in Jerusalem and would have been brought to the celebration. Even though these men wouldn't remember Josiah's Passover, they would remember the days that followed. These five children would grow up during the glory years of Judah and be deeply impacted by Josiah's reign. Being from the royal house, Daniel, Shadrach, Meshach, and Abednego would also have known Jeremiah and probably been taught directly by him. Ezekiel would have at least known about Jeremiah and likely heard him speak.

―――

Josiah's goal was to reunite the kingdom under God. He succeeded in reuniting the kingdom briefly; however, with only a few exceptions, like those mentioned above, he failed to turn the hearts of the people back to Yahweh. Josiah's most significant act was to renew the covenant, but even that was largely unsuccessful. A few years later, Jeremiah's message from God was that the people had broken the covenant again and "*returned to the sins of their ancestors*" (Jeremiah 11:10, see also 11:1–17). In their hearts, the people said, "*It's no use! I love foreign gods, and I must go after them*" (Jeremiah 2:25).

At a time when the people were at their worst in rebellion against God, God sent Jeremiah to warn them, and Josiah to model true faith for them. They enjoyed thirteen years of God's blessing. It was an easy time for them to return to God—a time when His goodness was on display and His judgement delayed. But the hearts of the people did not want God. Today, we also live in a time of mercy and delayed judgement. Sometimes we may wish that God would just judge our culture, but God is calling us, His church, to be glad that we have time to model faith to our neighbours, like Josiah did. Perhaps we'll have a chance, like Jeremiah, to share our faith with someone who later becomes a Daniel or Ezekiel, or maybe in our time there will be a larger revival that will bring our nation back to God. We must be faithful and not lose hope while we are living in the "now" of God's mercy.

For more than a decade, life was good. Jeremiah continued to bring God's warnings to both Judah and all the nations around them. He continued to prophesy that judgement was coming, but he prayed that the people would accept God's mercy. He and Josiah worked tirelessly to purify the nation; however, not everyone was happy. Members of Jeremiah's own village felt that he was going too far and that he had to be stopped.

One day, God told Jeremiah to go to the local potter's house to watch him work, and then God would give him a message. He saw the potter start to make a jar from a lump of clay, but there was an imperfection in it, so he pounded it back into a lump and started again. Then God spoke to Jeremiah and told him that people were like that clay, and God was the potter. He might start to do one thing with them and then change His mind and start over, doing something different. Specifically, God had begun to shape the nation for judgement, but if they repented, He would relent and reshape them for mercy. He told Jeremiah to tell the people, "*Look! I am preparing a disaster for you and devising a plan against you. So turn from your evil ways ...*" (Jeremiah 18:11). But God also told Jeremiah what to say if they rejected His offer. He was to warn them that destruction was coming that would lead to the end of the priesthood and the temple (Jeremiah 18:1–17).

This was the last straw for some of his fellow priests and even members of his own family from Anathoth. They heard what Jeremiah had proclaimed, but rather than repent and be forgiven, they became angry that he had prophesied that God would destroy the temple and the priesthood with it. They determined to kill him, but God revealed their plot to Jeremiah, and he was able to escape.

Afterwards, Jeremiah complained that God didn't judge the wicked quickly enough, and that they'd been leading him along as if he was a lamb to be sacrificed. Jeremiah didn't realize that in this way he was the example of the suffering Christ. One day, one of Jesus's closest companions would turn on Him (Matthew 26:23), and He would be led like a lamb to the slaughter (Isaiah 53:7). In both the message of the potter and the symbolism of the plot against Jeremiah, the overwhelming love of God was revealed (Jeremiah 18:18–23, 11:18–23, 12:1–6). Jeremiah wanted swift justice for his enemies while at the same time desiring that God forgive the nation as a whole. God gently reminded him that justice was best left for God to decide. We too must be slow to anger with our enemies and remember that the same God who has reshaped our lives for mercy because He loves us also loves our enemies. His desire is to reshape them as well.

<hr />

Another time, Jeremiah had to confront the pride of the people, who thought that they didn't need Yahweh. God told Jeremiah to buy a new linen belt and wear it as a sign for the people. Just like us, people 2,600 years ago took pride in how they looked. A fancy sash was like putting on a new Armani suit. The rich would wear these and walk with a bit of a swagger in their step. It would have been somewhat out of step for Jeremiah to put on high fashion, but he bought and wore the belt until enough people had noticed. Then God told him to go and hide the belt in a rocky crevice. He did this, and no doubt the people noticed that as well, and maybe asked where his belt was. After some months had passed, God sent him to retrieve it, but it was rotted and ruined. Then the message came from God, and Jeremiah went back to the city and held out his belt for the people to see. He told them that just as it was ruined, Yahweh would ruin the pride of Judah and Jerusalem. Just like the people were proud of their fancy clothes, they were also proud of their false gods and didn't see the need for the true creator. Yahweh had once been proud to show off His chosen people, but now they were stained with their disobedience and were disintegrating like the sash (Jeremiah 13:1–11).

If that picture wasn't clear enough, God instructed Jeremiah to tell them that just like wineskins were made to hold wine, in their disobedient state, the people were only fit to hold the wine of God's wrath. God was getting ready to make the people spiritually drunk and destroy them (Jeremiah 13:12–14). But even as the words of judgement were spoken, God again offered mercy, saying, "*Give glory to the Lord your God before He brings the darkness ...*" (Jeremiah 13:16a). Jeremiah pleaded with the people as much as God did. He told them, "*If you do not listen, I will weep in secret because of your pride ...*" (Jeremiah 13:17a, see Jeremiah 13:15–27).

Jeremiah was learning about the broken heart of God and how it replaces the desire to see God's judgement. He shared in God's sorrow, like a father watching a prodigal son turn against him. Ultimately, God would prove His love through Jesus's death while we were still sinners (Romans 5:8). Today, God calls us to join Him in weeping for the lost and extending to them the same call to repentance that Jeremiah extended to his neighbours. As we do, we must also watch our own lives to ensure that we're not too proud to accept God's correction.

Proverbs tells us that pride precedes destruction (Proverb 16:18), but it can be easy to fall into this sin. We want to feel that we're good, so we convince ourselves that our lives are under control and we don't need God's help for everything we do. Before we know it, we can become spiritually proud, just like the unsaved who believe they don't need God. We must remind ourselves that our own righteousness is no better than Jeremiah's rotting sash, and it's nothing to be proud of.

———◦———

Another way God had commanded the people to honour Him was to set aside time for Him. One day each week, the Sabbath, was to be holy to the Lord, and no work was to be done on it. The people had not obeyed this command, so Jeremiah was sent to again offer mercy. His message this time was that if the people would set aside the Sabbath for God, they would never be driven out of Jerusalem. However, if they didn't listen, the gates of the city would be burned (Jeremiah 17:19–27). The intent of the Sabbath isn't just to refrain from working but to focus on God and spend time with Him. It provides a picture of resting in the complete work of Jesus and not relying on our works to save us. This was again an invitation for the people to come back to their creator.

Today, the Sabbath has been expanded into a way of life. We are always to be in communion with God and to never stop praying (I Thessalonians 5:17). We have been adopted into God's family, but do we spend time with our Father? As we do, we give God a chance to speak into our lives. Then He can guide our path and keep us from temptation. We need to press in with God and encourage each other as Jeremiah did. He spent the years he had with King Josiah living out his faith and teaching the king's sons and relatives about their God so that they wouldn't just observe the Sabbath but would know why they were taking time out for their creator.

While Jeremiah was busy caring for the souls of the people, Josiah was concerned about their physical safety and protecting them from the threat of Assyria. Judah was a small, unconquered island in the Assyrian Empire, and Josiah wanted to keep it that way. In the second half of Josiah's reign, wars began again between Assyria and Babylon. These had kept the Assyrians' focus near to home and not on the far edges of their empire. That was the way Josiah liked it. The Babylonians had already taken the Assyrian capital of Nineveh a few years earlier, forcing the Assyrians back to Haran. Now Haran had fallen too. However, this time the armies of Egypt answered the call for help and rode to the aid of the Assyrians to recapture Haran. In Josiah's mind, this alliance threatened the safety of Judah, because if Assyria, with Egypt's aid, was successful in pushing Babylon back, they might regain their strength and start to reassert their power in their extended empire. However, Pharaoh had to march past Judah to get his troops to Haran, so Josiah decided to go to war against Egypt and stop them from getting past, or at least weaken their army before they did.

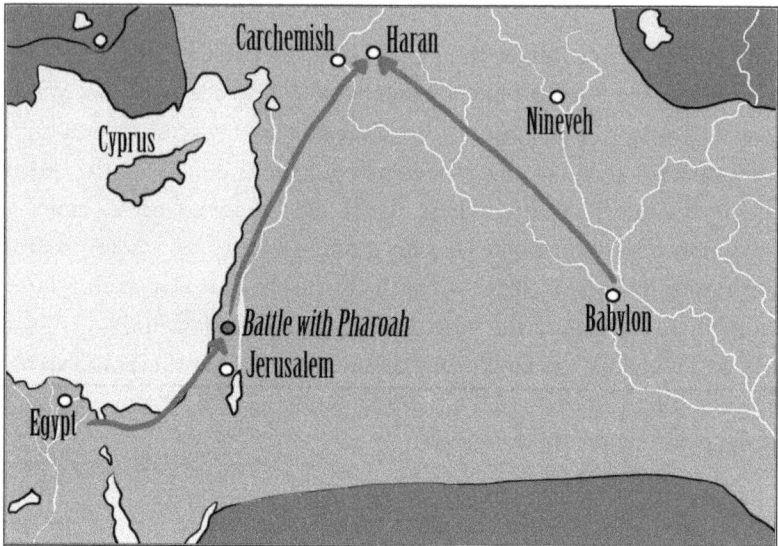

This was a foolish move, and Pharaoh warned Josiah not to do it, but Josiah refused to turn back, and he engaged Pharaoh's armies just north of Jerusalem. He was mortally wounded in the battle. He did get back to Jerusalem, but he died shortly afterwards (2 Kings 23:29–30; 2 Chronicles 35:20–24).

The depth of Jeremiah's love for Josiah was displayed in the lament he wrote for his friend, the king (2 Chronicles 35:25). With this lament and the burial of Josiah, the golden age ended suddenly. We never know how long we have before our time or someone else's will end. This had been an era in which God, near to the people, was calling them gently. We must make sure that we don't waste the opportunities we have to share Christ with those we know. We won't always have a chance to introduce people to the God of love.

I had a dear friend who found it hard to believe in a loving God, given the suffering he'd witnessed in his life. When he was diagnosed with terminal cancer, I determined to see him at least once a week and look for an opportunity to share Jesus's love with him. He had always stopped me in the past, but I thought that his condition might soften his heart. The first Saturday that I stopped by, he hadn't yet been told how much time he had, but he thought it would be a few years. I didn't try to share my faith, because it seemed like the wrong time. That next week he called me to say that the oncologist had met with him and told him that the end was very near, and he had only a month left. He understandably wanted to focus on his family and wasn't going to be seeing anyone else.

I was heartbroken and prayed that God would grant me one more opportunity to speak to my friend. I asked Him to forgive me for not having shared with him during the previous visit. Later, my wife asked his wife if they would like a meal, so we dropped one by that Saturday. On Sunday, we went to pick up the dishes. When my friend heard us at the door, he said he wanted to see us. He came out of the bedroom, and we had fifteen minutes together. By the grace of God, I had a second chance to speak to him. I held his hand and prayed for him and told him that he just needed to open his heart to Jesus. Rather than stop us, as he had in the past, he smiled and thanked us and told us that we were always welcome.

Three days later, he passed at home. Even when he first knew he was dying, he had no idea that he only had a few weeks left. I can't say if my friend accepted Jesus or not, but I do know that God heard my prayers and, through my wife and I, offered him mercy one last time. I am eternally grateful that I didn't waste that opportunity. Unless God tells me otherwise, I assume that I will meet him again in heaven.

Chapter Four

EGYPT IN CHARGE

T hings unravelled quickly after the death of the king. Josiah's attack had at least somewhat delayed and weakened Pharaoh. Pharaoh still made it to Haran, but he was either too late or too weakened to ultimately turn the tide. At the end of the battle, the Babylonians still held the city, and the Assyrian Empire was forced still farther back to Carchemish where, a few years later, they would make their last stand. Josiah had been hoping for this outcome, but he hadn't realized that the Babylonians would soon turn out to be a more powerful enemy than the Assyrians.

Pharaoh returned home, through Judah, a very angry man. While he'd been gone, the people of Judah had buried their king, mourned him, and made his second eldest son, Jehoahaz, king in his place. Jehoahaz was twenty-three years old. He was an interesting choice, since he wasn't the first-born. Perhaps either the older son or his mother were less desirable for some reason. Jehoahaz took the throne for three months, during which time Pharaoh went to Haran, battled, lost, and returned home. In his short time on the throne, Jehoahaz turned the clock back on all his father's reforms (2 Kings 23:32). It seems that he and his brothers had secretly never supported the return to faith in Yahweh that their father enforced. Perhaps the population in general, unhappy with Josiah's religious direction, had lobbied Josiah's sons to reverse things when the time came. Well, the time had come, and Jehoahaz did not waste the opportunity.

As Pharaoh was returning, Jehoahaz battled him at Riblah, a city near the northernmost border of the Northern Kingdom. For Jehoahaz to engage Pharaoh there, he would have had to rush out to him. Apparently, Jehoahaz wanted to finish the war his father had started. He thought that Pharaoh and his armies would have been weakened enough that he could press his advantage and get revenge for his father's death. We don't know for sure that this was his reasoning, but it would explain why he went all the way north to Riblah when Pharaoh was going to have to pass much closer to Jerusalem on his return home to Egypt.

Even though Pharaoh's armies were tired and depleted after their loss, Pharaoh was still a seasoned general, and Jehoahaz was just an impatient, hot-tempered young man. Pharaoh captured him and took him to Egypt, where he stayed until his death. When Pharaoh arrived in Jerusalem on his way home, he appointed Josiah's first-born son to be the king of Judah under Egypt's control. To ensure that it was clear that Egypt was now in charge, he changed the king's name to Jehoiakim and demanded tribute, which Jehoiakim had to raise from taxes on the people. Judah was no longer a free country but a vassal state occupied by its enemies.

Jeremiah watched this change occur over three short months. First, the country was free and under submission to God. Then his friend King Josiah was killed. Next, Josiah's son turned against God. A short time later, he was captured and the country came under Egyptian rule, paying tribute to Pharaoh. No doubt Jeremiah had advised Jehoahaz against his courses of action, but to no avail.

Sometimes we must watch the ones we care about make terrible life choices—or worse, terrible spiritual choices. God doesn't promise that they'll do the right thing if we pray hard enough. I'm sure Jeremiah prayed continually for Jehoahaz, a young man to whom he had tried to teach the ways of the Lord. He likely wept in secret for him too. But Jeremiah couldn't overrule Jehoahaz's free will any more than we can overrule the free will of those we love. We can only tell them what God says in His Word and let them know that we're praying for them. Then we must wait to see what God will do. If we're faithful in that, then whatever follows is not ours to decide but is between God and our loved ones.

On the other hand, we may sometimes be like Jehoahaz, acting outside the will of God. If so, we need to carefully consider the advice of the "Jeremiahs," or spiritual leaders, God has placed in our lives. We're likely not leading a country to abandon God like he did, but we still may do things that are against God's will without even realizing it. Some sins can slip into our lives unnoticed by us but clearly seen by others in our family or church. It could be greed, pride, anger, or holding a grudge. Or perhaps we indulge in sinful behaviour that we know is wrong, but we try to convince ourselves that God's not really concerned about our small indiscretions. God will use those around us to call us to holiness if we let Him.

Several years ago, my church offered an adult Bible study for people who wanted to examine their lives and motivations. It was structured for all believers, whether they were strong in their faith or had a lot of areas of struggle with the Lord. The intent was for the strong believers to lead by sharing their own struggles and encouraging the others. This required a great deal of honesty. I remember saying to several people that I thought it was a great idea, but I didn't sign up for it. We ran it several times, and it wasn't until the third round that I finally agreed to participate. It was surprising how much God had to say to me when I finally allowed myself to be vulnerable and listen.

———◆———

Once Jehoiakim was in control, Jeremiah had a fresh opportunity to advise the new king. But Jehoiakim would have nothing to do with it. He was as bent on leading the people back to pagan worship as his brother had been. Early in his reign, most likely to show Jeremiah that he was serious and wouldn't continue to follow the laws of Yahweh, the king vented his wrath against Uriah.

Uriah was a prophet like Jeremiah who also prophesied against Jerusalem and Judah, saying that they would be destroyed because of the sins of the people. When King Jehoiakim heard about it, he was determined to have Uriah put to death. But Uriah was warned of the plot, possibly by Jeremiah himself, and he fled to hide in Egypt. The king wouldn't let him go, so he sent a contingent to Egypt to capture and bring Uriah back. Since Judah was now part of the Egyptian Empire, they had the support of the Egyptian state to flush Uriah out, so they soon had him back in Jerusalem. When he stood for sentencing, Jehoiakim had him killed on the spot. This was intended to send a message to Jeremiah that there was no longer any hope of a return to the religious policies of Josiah (Jeremiah 26:20–23).

Jehoiakim made a mistake that many governments have made in the past. He supposed that true believers can be intimidated into giving up their convictions. Some believers may falter, of course, but if we trust in God, He will make us fearless. True believers have been persecuted at different times and places throughout history, but God's truth has found a voice in the midst of persecution. No matter what the future holds, or how many governments may oppose the church of God, we can be strong like Uriah and Jeremiah.

Jeremiah knew that Yahweh was his rock. Less than a year after the death of his friend Uriah, he was back at the temple reviewing all his prophecies of the past (Jeremiah 26:1–19). He told the people that if they turned from their evil ways, God would relent and not inflict the disaster He was planning. But if they wouldn't listen, Jerusalem and the temple would be destroyed.

In response to this message, the people seized him. They summoned the officials and demanded that they decree the death penalty on Jeremiah, just as it had been done to Uriah. Jeremiah's defence was bold. He told the officials that Yahweh had sent him to prophesy all these things, but that even now they could repent, obey God, and receive His mercy. Then he told them to do whatever they felt was right, but he warned them that if they killed him, they would be guilty of innocent blood. During the debate over Jeremiah's life, the prophet discovered that he wasn't without friends. Ahikam supported him, and God changed the minds of the people so that he'd be spared. He was, however, forbidden from coming to the temple to preach ever again (Jeremiah 36:5).

Where do we find the strength to fearlessly follow God like Jeremiah did? It can be found only in His presence. Knowing that God is by our side puts the threats around us into perspective. Jeremiah knew that his life was irrelevant compared to obedience to God. But this isn't something we can learn by studying the Bible; rather, we comprehend it through experience as we spend time talking with the Lord and getting to know Him.

———— ⬦ ————

As the war between Babylon and Assyria continued, Prince Nebuchadnezzar decided that he needed to prevent Egypt and its allies from coming to support Assyria again, so hesmoved his armies down into Judah in the third year of Jehoiakim's reign. As he arrived at Jerusalem, he demanded allegiance and sieged the city (Daniel 1:1). Jehoiakim held out long enough that Pharaoh wouldn't be able to accuse him of dereliction of duty to Egypt, but then he surrendered. His was already a vassal state, so he reasoned that it would be no worse under Babylon than it was under Egypt. He also expected that his nation's status would be resolved later in the imminent battle between Egypt and Babylon.

When Jehoiakim opened the city gates to let him in, Nebuchadnezzar took some prisoners captive to Babylon. Among them were Daniel, Shadrach, Meshach, and Abednego. At this time, however, Nebuchadnezzar received word that his father had died, so instead of pressing the attack against Egypt, he rode across the desert back to Babylon to secure his throne. Jehoiakim was technically left as a vassal of Babylon, but he wasn't altogether sure if his loyalty should go to King Nebuchadnezzar or if it should remain with Egypt, whose armies were still much closer.

———— ⬦ ————

A year later, Egypt again went to the aid of the remnant of the Assyrian Empire. This time, the battle was at Carchemish, and the defeat was complete. King Nebuchadnezzar and the armies of Babylon took over the Assyrian Empire, and the Babylonians were now firmly in charge. What was left of the Egyptian army slunk dejectedly home, and Judah was left wondering what it all meant for them. With Assyria defeated, Egypt's power reduced, and Babylon so far away, perhaps they could be free again. The false prophets, with whom the king had surrounded himself, began to preach about the coming glory of Jehoiakim's reign.

In counter-point to the message of the false prophets, Jeremiah began preaching through the countryside. Normally if someone had something to say, they would go to the temple, where all the people would gather. However, since he was under a restraining order not to go near the temple, Jeremiah went to the places where the people lived. It is noteworthy that he obeyed the unjust ruling of the king in this case. He didn't go back to the temple but found other ways to still obey God and faithfully proclaim His message. As Christians, we're called to obey the laws of the land, even when they're unjust, as long as we're not being forced to disobey God. There have been rulings against Christians who have spoken for God in public spaces, abortion clinics, and other venues. They have at times been barred from returning to those places. We need to pray for wisdom as to how God would have us comport ourselves when the courts turn against righteousness. We must not lose our godly passion to see justice done, but we should prayerfully consider how to proceed.

In his preaching tour, Jeremiah reminded the people that he'd been preaching for twenty-three years, but no one had been listening (Jeremiah 25:1–3). He told them that he and the true prophets before him had offered God's mercy to the people, but they hadn't turned back to Yahweh to be spared (Jeremiah 25:4–6). Therefore, God had raised up a servant in Nebuchadnezzar, King of Babylon, who would come and destroy Judah and all the countries in the region (Jeremiah 25:7–11). In direct contrast to the false prophets around him, and under threat of death, Jeremiah preached his message of judgement and destruction once again.

But twenty-three years earlier, God had promised Jeremiah that he would plant nations as well as uproot them. After waiting for what must have seemed a lifetime, Jeremiah was given a message of hope for Judah. The punishment would not last forever. After seventy years, Babylon would be dealt with and the exile of Judah would come to an end. This was the first time that Jeremiah prophesied about the return. Up to this point, he had only known that the land would be destroyed. Finally, he knew it would be rebuilt!

There are times in our lives when God removes things that we rely on. Often it's something we know is wrong, like an addictive behaviour we've used to manage the pain in our souls. Sometimes, though, it may be something good. It could be a job that has provided for us but now stands in the way of God's plans for where we should be. Whatever the case, when God removes supports from our lives, He always starts re-building. As we submit to Him, He replaces those things with new life, and He calls us closer to Himself.

This process won't happen quickly, or on our timetable. Jeremiah's promise wasn't something with which the people could glibly console themselves; seventy years is a long time. When we walk through the hard times in life, God doesn't often revive us in two or three days, like many false voices will try to tell us (Hosea 6:2). Rather, He leads us through much longer processes in our lives until we experience real repentance, or true trust, or deeper love ... whatever His objective may be. We need to trust the promise of renewal in the dark times and hold on to God as He works at His pace in us.

As a follow-up to his preaching tour on the coming of Nebuchadnezzar the Destroyer, Jeremiah got his scribe, Baruch, to write down all the prophecies and messages that Jeremiah had ever given (Jeremiah 36:1–3). This was the first copy of the book of Jeremiah. Jeremiah could have written it himself, but a scribe was employed to create a scroll worthy of the message. They were trained in calligraphy and attention to the layout and presentation. This is the first mention of Baruch, but he is seen throughout the rest of Jeremiah's life, working with and supporting the prophet.

Jeremiah then asked the unthinkable of Baruch. He told him that God wanted to remind the people of all the messages He had spoken through Jeremiah. This reminder was intended to give the people another opportunity to repent and be saved from the coming destruction. The scroll needed to be read to the people at the temple; however, since Jeremiah couldn't go to the temple, he asked Baruch to go instead and read the scroll (Jeremiah 36:4–7). Baruch was to offer the people God's mercy. As he was acutely aware of what had happened to Uriah just a few years earlier for delivering this same kind of message, Baruch feared for his life.

God instructed Jeremiah to do this just after Nebuchadnezzar had defeated Assyria at Carchemish, but the instruction was to wait until a day of fasting had been declared. This would bring as many people as possible to the temple, and they would be the most open to hearing from God.

Baruch prepared the scroll and then they waited for more than a year. While they waited, Baruch complained to God about His unfair treatment (Jeremiah 45:1–5). He was terrified of the task he'd been given and didn't want to risk his life that way. He told God that it wasn't fair to add sorrow to his pain. Life was hard enough without having to seek trouble. So God gave Jeremiah a message for his friend. Jeremiah told Baruch that during a time when God was judging the world and destroying kingdoms, it was inappropriate for Baruch to seek any blessing for himself. Nevertheless, despite the coming destruction, God would allow Baruch to escape, but only with his life.

That seems a harsh message, and it goes against what we like to hear. We want to know that we'll have everything we think we need, such as a home, a retirement, and grandchildren to play with. Shouldn't our faithful service to God be repaid by His blessings on our lives? But here we see God promising Baruch that even though he would lose everything else, he wouldn't be killed. We need to understand God's priorities for us. He's aware of the number of hairs on our head and is concerned with every aspect of our lives (Luke 12:7); however, He's more concerned about the condition of our souls than our transitory earthly comfort. He has made us a promise similar to what he made to

Baruch: His presence with us on earth and eternal life (John 10:29). But we must align ourselves with God's priorities. We must not consider our physical comfort to be the goal of our lives but rather let our love for God drive us. And from there, we must reach out to the lost.

Bitterness, anger, and fear are all related. When we hold on to hurts from the past and refuse to let God help us forgive, we become bitter. When we believe someone is hurting us in the present and we don't give it to God, we become angry. When we don't trust God to take care of us in the future, we become afraid. All three come from a lack of faith that God is in control and that whatever we lose in this life is in His hands. God's gift to Baruch was to take away everything he had. Once we accept that nothing we have is ours, then we have nothing to lose. We can no longer be bitter about what others have done to us in the past, because anything they did was against God, not against us. We can no longer be angry about the hurts of the present, because we have nothing that can be taken from us. And we can't be afraid or intimidated by others, as our future is secure in Christ. We need to submit our wealth, homes, retirement funds, families, and even our lives to God's will. Then we will be fearless and say with the psalmist, *"The Lord is with me; I will not be afraid. What can mere mortals do to me?"* (Psalm 118:6).

Handing our lives over to God is not an easy transition. Graciously, God gave Baruch more than a year to work through this lesson and find his courage in God. Although we often feel pressured to rush into things, God does not. It wasn't until after Nebuchadnezzar had consolidated his power in the second year of his reign that he began to cast his gaze back at the edges of the old Assyrian Empire, and the King of Judah began to worry. Jehoiakim called a fast for the people to seek divine favour. The people poured into Jerusalem, to the temple, to pray. There they were met by Baruch, reading the scroll of all of Jeremiah's prophecies and sermons and offering them a way to God's forgiveness and mercy. This was the very thing for which they were fasting and praying (Jeremiah 36:8–10).

The common people listened to Jeremiah's previous messages, and the local officials heard them too. The officials were afraid of the disaster that was proclaimed, and they decided that the king must know about these prophecies. They realized that this may not be well received in court, so they told Baruch to go and hide with Jeremiah (Jeremiah 36:11–19).

For the king, however, who had grown up with Jeremiah, this was nothing new; he had heard it all before. Since it was winter and there was a chill in the air, the king was sitting by a fire as the scroll was read to him. Each time a few columns were read, he cut them off the roll and burned them in the fire. When the entire scroll was burned, Jehoiakim called for Jeremiah and Baruch to be arrested, but they couldn't be found (Jeremiah 36:20–26). Because of the relationship that Jehoiakim had had with Jeremiah before Josiah's death, he didn't pursue him the way he'd pursued Uriah. God used this special relationship Jeremiah had with Jehoiakim and his brother to continue to protect Jeremiah.

While they were hiding, Jeremiah and Baruch made another copy of the scroll. Then Jeremiah sent a message to King Jehoiakim and told him that since he wouldn't believe the prophecies from Yahweh, he wouldn't be allowed to have a dynasty. His son wouldn't remain on the throne after Jehoiakim's death; furthermore, Jehoiakim would not be given respect in death, but his body would be thrown out of the city and exposed to rot. Meanwhile, the people had taken their cue from the king. If he wasn't afraid, they wouldn't be afraid either. They also ignored God's call to repentance. Because of this, Jeremiah confirmed that Nebuchadnezzar the Destroyer would certainly come to destroy Jerusalem (Jeremiah 36:27–32).

Soon after Baruch's reading, Jehoiakim decided to take the chance that Babylon was too far away to be bothered coming back to Judah now that Egypt was no longer a threat to them. His false prophets reinforced this thought, which emboldened him to rebel against Babylon. Nebuchadnezzar, however, did come back to Jerusalem. His armies were powerful, and the people resubmitted without much of a fight. Nebuchadnezzar confirmed his hold on Jehoiakim. He was no longer a servant of Egypt but of Babylon. Then Nebuchadnezzar took more captives from the richest people, including members of the royal family. The kingdom of Judah was allowed to continue to exist under Nebuchadnezzar as part of the new empire (2 Kings 24:1–7). This too was God's mercy to allow them more time. It should have confirmed all of Jeremiah's words and brought the people to repentance. Even though they had suffered defeat, there was still time to avoid destruction.

Chapter Five

BABYLON AND REBELLION

G od often speaks in parables and pictures. He did this through the prophets of the Old Testament in the same way that Jesus did when He was on earth.

After both the king and the people had rejected His last offer of mercy and forgiveness, God allowed Nebuchadnezzar to confirm his control over the country. To help the people understand what had happened, God sent them another message through Jeremiah.

At that time there was a family of nomadic shepherds living in Judah. As a clan, they were called Rekabites, after their most prominent ancestor. Normally, they didn't enter the city except to do business for a day and then immediately leave. However, with Nebuchadnezzar's armies running throughout the land, they came into Jerusalem for safety. Jeremiah invited them to share a meal with him in the rooms of a righteous man whose family lived and served at the temple. This would have been as close as Jeremiah's restraining order permitted him to come to the temple.

Jeremiah then offered the family wine, even though he already knew they wouldn't drink it (Jeremiah 35:1–5). When the Rekabites declined the wine, they explained that their forefather had forbidden them from drinking wine or settling in one place. For generations they had obeyed these family rules until Nebuchadnezzar invaded and they had been forced into the city to seek safety (Jeremiah 35:6–11).

Then Jeremiah drew out the object lesson. In contrast to this family's obedience to their forefather, Yahweh had repeatedly told His people what was expected of them, and for generation after generation they had disobeyed His laws. God had told the people to reject false gods and return to Him, the one true God. He had also promised that He would let them live in safety if they obeyed, but they continued to ignore His pleas. Now all the disasters pronounced against God's people would come on them (Jeremiah 35:12–17).

Although Jeremiah declared God's pronouncements for the future, he preached more than he prophesied. When the Law of Moses had been found twenty years earlier, Jeremiah had studied it. In it, Moses had predicted that when the people turned from Yahweh, He would send disasters on them, eventually exiling them from the land altogether. Jeremiah used the same language in his preaching, showing that he was preaching from the Law. Then his prophecies added the specifics of how God would do it, such as with the disaster coming from the north or Nebuchadnezzar executing God's judgement. Even if the people didn't know if Jeremiah was speaking for God in his prophecies, they would absolutely know that Jeremiah was preaching from the Law and not his own imagination. Knowing this, they should have listened to him and obeyed God.

Jeremiah's example of the Rekabites' obedience was given to stir the people to repentance. It was a severe warning that the time before the judgement was very short.

After chastising the people, Jeremiah gave the Rekabites a promise too. He told them that God would ensure their line would always continue with descendants who were faithful to God. This message was for everyone. God was looking for faithful worshippers who would be with Him forever (John 4:23–24).

When we centre our lives on Jesus and focus on doing His will, we're given the same promise God gave the Rekabites: we will live with God forever. But if we ignore God's Word, given to us in the Bible, we have already left God's presence. When God tells us that we're falling short of His Law, we have a choice. We can submit and live in His presence, or we can merely listen to the Word but not obey it and change our behaviour. If we do that, we rob ourselves of the freedom to live in His presence (James 1:22–25).

Heaven is not a topic for funerals only. It's a place where we will be face to face with our creator, God the Father, and our Saviour, Jesus Christ. Our life on earth is intended to be a time in which we get to know and trust God through both the blessings and the hard times. That brings heaven into our lives now. Eternal life is knowing the Father and Jesus (John 17:3). Many Christians are afraid of death when the time comes, but the better we know who we're going to see, the less we'll fear death. Eternal communion with God was the promise to the Rekabites for their faithfulness.

For the next few years, life settled into a routine. The state of Judah was allowed to continue as long as its people paid taxes to Babylon. They did, but they also continued to ignore the messages of Jeremiah. Since nothing worse seemed to happen, they felt that perhaps he'd been wrong. There was, however, the annoying issue of being subjugated to Babylon.

King Jehoiakim tried to decide what would be better: being tied to Babylon, or to Egypt. Then he saw what he thought was a way to get out from under both foreign powers. What if Egypt, Judah, and the other neighbouring countries stood up to Babylon together? Perhaps they could form an alliance to keep Nebuchadnezzar from coming back. This would be to the mutual benefit of all nations in the area. So with some assurances from Egypt's Pharaoh, Jehoiakim once again rebelled.

Through Jeremiah, however, God had been clear that Nebuchadnezzar had been sent to chastise the people for their disobedience. Rebelling against him was therefore the same as rebelling against God. There was still time to set things right and live under God's mercy rather than His judgement, but that now meant that the people would have to submit to Nebuchadnezzar.

When the news of this latest rebellion first came to Jeremiah, the Lord gave him a message for the king. Jeremiah was sent directly to the palace to deliver God's proclamation. For anyone else who did not have his special relationship with the royal family, this would have been a death sentence, but God was protecting Jeremiah. The message had four parts. First was a list of behaviours that a king should exhibit. Then there were messages about Jehoiakim's brother, who was already exiled in Egypt, Jehoiakim himself, and finally Jehoiakim's son.

Jeremiah told Jehoiakim that a king should protect the victims of crime. He should not take advantage of the defenceless, such as immigrants, widows, and orphans. He should not have innocent people killed. The prophet Uriah wasn't mentioned but must have been on the tip of Jeremiah's tongue. The picture of a righteous king was a clear accusation against Jehoiakim, showing how he fell sadly short in these and many other virtues. But with the truth came the choice again. If the king would repent and do all this, there would be kings in Jerusalem forever. But if the monarchy remained corrupt, the palace would be cut up and burned and the kingdom would be lost. Jehoiakim was reminded that he had committed to keep the covenant and the Law of Moses when he had been a lad of twelve. He was told not to forsake it as an adult (Jeremiah 22:1–9).

Then Jeremiah told his listeners that they should not hope to see Jehoahaz ever again. Jehoiakim's brother had been taken to Egypt almost a decade earlier, and with a possible alliance in the making, there was talk about Egypt releasing him. Jeremiah affirmed that this was not going to happen. Jehoahaz would die in Egypt (Jeremiah 22:10–12).

The next message was the most personal yet. Jeremiah rebuked Jehoiakim for having refurbished his palace with slave labour. He contrasted this with Jehoiakim's father, who had not burdened the people but had rather defended the poor and needy. Jehoiakim was too eager to cheat people and kill any who got in his way. The prophet told him for the second time that when he died, he would not be mourned, but rather his body would be thrown outside the city. He also told the king that the alliance he was building would fail, and the rebellion would not succeed. His stubborn refusal to listen, which had been a fault of the king since his youth, would end in his ruin (Jeremiah 22:13–23). Finally, to round off the rebuke, Jeremiah told the king that his son

Jehoiachin, who was now fifteen years old, would be exiled with his mother to Babylon and never return (Jeremiah 22:24–30).

Talk about an earful! Jehoiakim was told that he was evil, his brother would never be released from Egypt, he would fail in his rebellion, he would die and not be mourned, and his wife and son would be exiled and never return, so he would have no legacy. It's no wonder the king had grown to hate Jeremiah! And he must have hated Jeremiah even more when Nebuchadnezzar returned to wage war on Judah, and everything that was prophesied began to come to pass. All the countries that still held allegiances to Egypt would be subdued by Babylon during this campaign, and Egypt's armies would remain behind their own borders, leaving Judah defenceless.

God is very serious about how we relate to those weaker than us. The Old Testament contains many passages like this one, where God reserves some of His harshest judgements for those who abuse the poor and the defenceless. The people of God are to be fair and generous. This heart attitude will display itself in small things as well as large. It will come out in how we tip at restaurants or how we interact with the homeless. It will also be seen in what we do as a church to help our vulnerable brothers and sisters in Christ as well as those in our communities. The primary purpose of the church is to proclaim Christ and not to champion social action, but in proclaiming Jesus, it wouldn't hurt us to provide water for people without it in Africa, or homes in our community for unwed mothers, or low cost assisted living for the aging, or meals for the homeless. We should take care of the needy in the church first, as they are our family. Then let the generosity spill out to the world around us.

———— ❧ ————

It took some time for Babylon to coordinate their attack and bring an army down to Judah. Many battles were waged during the campaign to take over the region. In the end, Jehoiakim was captured in battle.

The Bible contains three different accounts of Jehoiakim's death, and at first they appear to contradict each other. Jeremiah had told him twice that he would be killed and his body would be left to rot outside the gates of Jerusalem without burial (Jeremiah 22:18–19, 36:30). Another account claims that he was buried with his ancestors (2 Kings 24:6). Finally, it's said that he was captured and bound to be taken to Babylon (2 Chronicles 36:6). When we see issues like this, we can rest assured that we can trust the Bible. Each passage had a different point to make, so they each told only part of the story. Jeremiah was focused on the punishment of Jehoiakim's sins. The account in 2 Kings merely summarized his life, and the passage in 2 Chronicles focused on the domination of Jehoiakim by Nebuchadnezzar. We can trust that the Bible is completely true and inspired by God, and we do not need to skirt around apparent problems.

Jehoiakim was taken in battle and bound in chains so that he could be deported to Babylon (2 Chronicles 36:6); however, before he left the area, Nebuchadnezzar needed to restructure the state of Judah, so he went to Jerusalem first. Hearing that his father had been captured and that Nebuchadnezzar was on his way to Jerusalem, Jehoiachin sealed the city against the armies of Babylon. This forced Nebuchadnezzar to siege the city, which was a costly annoyance. In his frustration, he had Jehoiakim killed and his body dumped against the walls of the city and left to rot. Jehoiachin now became king of a surrounded city, and he held out for one hundred days before surrendering (2 Chronicles 36:9).

When Nebuchadnezzar had come to Jerusalem before, he had taken some captives and demanded tribute. This time would make his previous actions seem like a visit from a friend. Nebuchadnezzar pillaged the city and the temple. He took the remaining seven thousand soldiers captive along with most of the royal family, including, as predicted, Jehoiachin and his mother. He also took all the richest citizens and craftsmen. Among the captives was Ezekiel, who would later become a prophet to the exiles. In the war that had lasted a few years, the country had seen hundreds of thousands killed, tens of thousands more taken into captivity, and more again fleeing to Egypt and other places in self-imposed exile before the coming of Nebuchadnezzar the Destroyer. The country was devastated.

When he was finished, Nebuchadnezzar renamed Josiah's third son "Zedekiah" and put him on the throne as a vassal king of a greatly diminished nation. He forced Zedekiah to swear an oath to Yahweh that he would serve Babylon faithfully (2 Chronicles 36:13). Finally, after the Babylonian armies had fully withdrawn, Zedekiah retrieved what was left of his brother Jehoiakim's body and buried it without any ceremony (2 Kings 24:6).

Jehoiakim had ruled as an evil man. He reinstituted the false religions that forced young men and women into prostitution. He stole from his subjects. He murdered the innocent and re-established infanticide in worship to Moloch. The Bible refers to Manasseh as the reason why God was determined to punish Judah (2 Kings 24:3–4). Manasseh had set the people on a path that had become a stronghold in the culture. Except for Josiah, all the kings after Manasseh followed in his steps. The people were never able to break away from the evil practices entrenched by Manasseh. Still, throughout Jeremiah's life, from Manasseh to Zedekiah, Yahweh continually offered the people a way to escape the coming judgement. Each time they refused, however, the consequences increased.

We find it hard to relate to kings like Jehoiakim. Most of us don't have the inclination or the opportunity to express the evil side of humanity the way he did. However, we may at times share his stubborn refusal to examine our lives and make course corrections where they're needed. We may not have Jeremiah correcting us, but do we listen to our spouse, our parents, our pastors, or our brothers and sisters in Christ when they point out our shortcomings? Or do we justify ourselves and imagine that everyone else's perception is skewed? We need a soft heart that listens for God's correction.

Jeremiah had first met the king as a young lad of twelve. He watched him go through the motions of dedicating his life to God during Josiah's Passover, when Jehoiakim was caught up in the moment with everyone else. Later, Jeremiah tutored him in the ways of God, but he observed Jehoiakim's lack of real devotion and his refusal to allow the truth to permeate and change his soul. As king, Jehoiakim rejected God's Law, which his father and Jeremiah had tried to teach him. Jeremiah could have gloated when Jehoiakim finally met his end, but Jeremiah's love was unfailing. His messages had delivered tough love, but always in hope of seeing Jehoiakim repent. In secret, Jeremiah had wept for this young man whom he thought of as a son, and he lamented his passing (Lamentations 2:22).

We are called to love people. There's no guarantee how they will respond, but we must pray for them and speak the truth to them just the same. Unfortunately, like Jeremiah, we must sometimes leave them, along with our broken hearts, in God's hands.

Chapter Six

ZEDEKIAH—THE EARLY YEARS

Zedekiah was the fourth king since Josiah's death, yet barely a decade had passed. All three of Josiah's sons and one of his grandsons had now sat on his throne. The kingdom had decayed through war, desertion, and deportations, so it was now an empty shell of what it had been under Zedekiah's father. But God wasn't finished with His people. There was still time for repentance and mercy, which He continued to offer through Jeremiah.

When Zedekiah was made king, he didn't pay any attention to the messages of God that Jeremiah preached. This was also true of Zedekiah's officials and nearly everyone who remained in the land. However, Zedekiah held a pagan belief that many people today also agree with. While he didn't think that God should be allowed to interfere in how he ran his life, he did think that God should bless it. So he sent a couple of his officials to Jeremiah to ask the prophet to pray for him and the country (Jeremiah 37:1–3).

This is incredibly audacious, yet it appears to be the default belief system of a large part of our society and even the church. We can be tempted to see God as a giant vending machine. We put in a few prayers and maybe a small donation, and out comes a promotion at work, or a raise, or a new house. However, the function of prayer is not to bend God's will to our control; rather, it helps us lay down our will in submission to His. Our heavenly Father is doing great things around us, and if we let Him, He will do great things in and through us. Through prayer, He invites us to participate in what He has already begun. Like a small child in a parent's workshop being asked to hold the end of a board the parent is cutting, we join with the Father in what He's doing—not because He needs us, but because He longs to share the experience with us. Prayer opens the door for us to enter God's workshop.

———— ✺ ————

Jeremiah wasn't fooled by Zedekiah's request. He didn't believe that there was going to be a change under the third son, but he prayed for king and kingdom anyway. He'd been doing that already, so he didn't need to be asked. However, God had a response for Zedekiah. Jeremiah was given a vision in which he saw two baskets of figs set in front of the temple, figuratively coming to God for a blessing. One was bursting with good figs while the other was full of rotten and inedible ones. The good figs represented the exiles, and Jeremiah was told that God would take care of them and give them a change of heart so that they would long to know Him. The rotten figs, however, symbolized King Zedekiah, his officials, and all the people who were left in Judah. God would destroy them by plague, famine, and sword (Jeremiah 24:1–10).

This was a pivotal message for the people, and it was the first prophecy to come without an option for mercy or hope. There was, of course, hope for the country, because the exiles, represented by the good figs, would return one day. But there was no offer of hope for those still in the land, represented by the bad figs. Coming as it did at the start of Zedekiah's reign and right after he had asked for his manipulative prayer, this message was intended to shock the king and the people. There would be no hope for them in their current state. It defined two groups, and if they remained in the bad basket, their only future would be destruction.

This doesn't mean that the option of mercy had been withdrawn. It would be offered many more times before the end, but Yahweh was trying to break through the rock-hard cover on His people's hearts. From this point on, the question would be which group the people wanted to be in: the one destined for destruction, or the one set aside for restoration.

Jeremiah preached about this vision to those in Jerusalem, and we can only imagine how much they detested his message. But he also had good news for the exiles, so he sent a letter to Babylon.

People constantly travelled between Jerusalem and Babylon to pay the tribute and get instructions from the Babylonian court, so it was easy to send a letter back to the exiles. In the letter, he told the people to settle down, build homes, marry, and have children. In a time of incredible upheaval and uncertainty, these basic human needs had been put on hold. Jeremiah reassured the exiles that, for them, the worst was over (Jeremiah 29:1–6). God may allow hardship in our lives for a time, but He also refreshes us. Sometimes, however, the door to refreshing is harder to open than we'd like.

Jeremiah next told them to pray for the peace of Babylon, because their lives were tied to it. That was a hard request. They had been ripped from their homes and lost everything. Most of them had watched loved ones murdered, and then they had to start life over again in a different country, learning a new language. After all that, Jeremiah told them to pray for those who had subjected them to it. But our lives are not only bound to those we love; they're bound to our enemies as well. In many ways, to pray for our enemies is to pray for ourselves. To free ourselves from hate, we must learn to forgive. To freely experience joy, we must do what we can to help them have joy. God created us as a race. As such, we're not individuals, but we draw our life from each other. We're physically the product of our parents and are born into a family. By extension, our bodies are part of the whole human family. In the same way, we're spiritually bound together. If our enemies prosper spiritually, we will too.

The literal meaning in Jeremiah's letter was an economic one. If Babylon's economy was blessed, the refugees would share in that financial boon. But as we see so often between the Old and New Testaments, the Old Testament shows a physical picture that has a spiritual truth behind it and is picked up in the New Testament. Jesus told us to pray for our enemies too (Matthew 5:44–45), and as we pray, by His grace, they may even become our friends (Jeremiah 29:7).

Part of Jeremiah's letter is well known and often quoted: "*'For I know the plans I have for you,' declares the Lord, 'plans to prosper you and not to harm you, plans to give you hope and a future'*" (Jeremiah 29:11). Do we understand the context of this message, and would we embrace it so quickly if we did? It was understood in Babylon, and the false prophets, both in Judah and among the refugees in Babylon, rejected it completely.

The false prophets told the people that God would soon bring them back to Jerusalem. They said that within two years, He would restore the glory of Judah and the temple. This beautiful verse of promise came with a warning against these prophets. There would be no return for another seventy years. This was why the people needed to settle down; they would be in Babylon for the long haul. The promise was made to let them know that God would restore His people, but they had to undergo a change of heart first. That process was going to take a generation or more to accomplish. Jeremiah told them that there would be no country to return to in the short term, because those who were left were disobedient and worthless, like a basket of rotten figs. Furthermore, those in exile were equally guilty, but God would remove the false prophets that were with them, and He would bring them back to Himself (Jeremiah 29:8–23).

This isn't a promise that God will remove all the hardships from our lives but that He will bless us in our suffering. This is a promise for the parents who have lost a child, that God will bless them in their grief. It's the promise for the person who prays for healing but remains sick, or for the spouse who prays for restoration of their marriage, but their partner leaves anyway. It's for the person who is heartbroken in their marriage and wants to leave, but God tells them that He will bless the marriage if they remain in it. It's for the worker who prays for favour and promotion but is passed over anyway. This isn't the easy way out, but the hard way through.

This isn't to say that we shouldn't pray for an end to our suffering. Those are good prayers. Zedekiah wanted prayer for the restoration of his people and his kingdom. That wasn't a bad thing to ask for, but he didn't really ask ... he insisted. When we ask, we must be ready to submit if the answer is "no." Even so, these verses give us one of the greatest promises in the Old Testament. They assure us of His blessings, even when God says "no" (2 Corinthians 12:7–8).

Often we want to go straight to God's blessings without learning His lessons. It's better for us to suffer and draw closer to God than to live with ease and drift away from Him. This message can be as hard for us to receive as it was for the exiles. We shouldn't think that they were immediately glad to hear that God had their future in His hands. The only message most of them heard was that they would be exiled for seventy years. God had to send them the prophet Ezekiel to drive this promise home, and it took time for them to get beyond God's "no" to see that Yahweh was promising to be with them and to bless them through the exile.

Jeremiah's letter didn't go unnoticed. Nebuchadnezzar had it read to him and was very pleased. He probably didn't take it seriously, but Jeremiah had encouraged the exiles not to cause problems but to submit to the Babylonian kingdom. What might or might not happen in seventy years didn't concern Nebuchadnezzar—he was only concerned that the new arrivals not cause him any further trouble. In this way, Jeremiah made a somewhat unexpected friend, who would continue to keep tabs on him and his prophecies over the next decade.

The false prophets in Babylon weren't as taken with the message. Two of them had been told they would shortly be burned alive by Nebuchadnezzar for lying in God's name and pretending to be prophets while leading immoral lives. A third one, Shemaiah, sent back a letter of his own to everyone in Jerusalem, including the high priest, Zephaniah. In it, he accused the high priest of dereliction of duty. Zephaniah had recently become the high priest to fill the hole left by the last high priest, who had been taken to Babylon in the deportation. Shemaiah's letter basically told him that he wasn't qualified unless he knew that it was his responsibility to have Jeremiah put in the stocks, because Jeremiah was a maniac pretending to be a prophet. However, God again protected Jeremiah. Zephaniah read the letter to him and sent Jeremiah's response back on his behalf. God's word for Shemaiah was that even though He was going to bless the exiles, Shemaiah would not be included in those blessings; rather, his family would decrease until there were none left (Jeremiah 29:24–32).

Whenever God plans a blessing, He leaves us free to decide if we will participate or withdraw from the sphere of His plans for us. In this case, Shemaiah was among those who were preaching that God would quickly bring the people back home. He told them not to settle down, since they wouldn't be in Babylon very long. It offended him that Jeremiah would suggest that they would have to suffer exile for seventy years. He figuratively removed himself from the bowl of good figs and joined King Zedekiah in the bowl of rotten figs.

When we're in a difficult circumstance, knowing that God is near and walking through it with us means that we don't have to suffer alone. The sorrows of life will come, but they will also pass. We must trust God, even when we feel exiled from His favour. When we feel far away from Him, we can be assured that His plan is to prosper our spirits and not harm us. We always have a future when we leave our lives in His hands.

Just as Shemaiah had rejected his position in the bowl of good figs, the people in Jerusalem would be given many more opportunities to leave the bowl of bad figs and join those who were going to be renewed by God. The bad news that we are sinners is intended to highlight our choice to turn from our sin. Likewise, when God disciplines us as His children, we can submit and draw closer to Him or resist and fall farther from His presence. Every event in our lives, both before we come to Christ and after, is an opportunity to chose to know Him better.

Jeremiah's prayer for Zedekiah and the delivery of God's message put Jeremiah in the worst position of his life. Although he had found an ally in Zephaniah, the high priest, he had turned almost everyone against him. Though he didn't waver in his faith in God, he was not un-affected either. Jeremiah settled into a deep depression. After a time, Yahweh comforted Jeremiah in a dream (Jeremiah 30:1–31:26).

The dream expanded on the return of the people, but it covered so much more than the promised event that was seventy years in the future. God spoke to Jeremiah about the destruction and rebuilding of the land. He spoke of retribution on the wicked and discipline for the people of God. But although it included the return that God had promised, it also included the greater fulfilment of the coming of the Messiah.

Jeremiah was shown Jesus on the throne of King David (Jeremiah 30:9). He saw the Messiah as a ruler who was close to the Father (Jeremiah 30:21). The dream showed him the suffering of God's people because of their sins, but it also showed him their repentance and the reconciliation between man and God. He saw God as our husband and also as our father. Then came the foretelling of the birth of Christ and the slaughter of the innocents (Jeremiah 31:15–16). But just after the prediction of the murder of these precious baby boys by Herod, God spoke comfort and hope. The Messiah would suffer too, but His work would be rewarded.

In Jeremiah's day, interaction with God was prescribed by rules that foreshadowed the relationship God wanted with us. People like Abraham, David, and Jeremiah walked in deep communion with God, but the depth of the relationship God was planning for all His people was not fully understood. In this dream, Jeremiah glimpsed the reckless love of God. The Messiah would be intimate with our sufferings and would meet us in them to draw us heavenward, so despite the catastrophic elements of the dream, when Jeremiah woke from it, he was refreshed (Jeremiah 31:26). The depression was lifted from him, and he could receive love from God once again.

As Jeremiah lay enraptured on his bed, God continued to speak to him about the new covenant that would come with the Messiah (Jeremiah 31:27–40). It would be a time when generational curses would be broken (Jeremiah 31:29–30). Children would be freed from the sins of their parents. God's law would not be external. In place of rules, we would internalize His law in our hearts and minds (Jeremiah 31:33).

We are living in the world that Jeremiah saw! His dream stretched through time and into eternity and heaven, but we now grasp the plan of salvation that he only saw from a distance. Just seeing it, however, gave him peace and hope in the midst of depression and despair. Whatever we face, the presence of Jesus is always with us. We can hold on to Him to find our peace in the storm.

Depression is a terrible state and sometimes may be more medical than emotional. Not only is there no shame in depression, but it is wise to consult a physician to determine if there are any physical causes for the depression. However, there are times when it strikes us because we're focused on our circumstances rather than on the God who is in control of those circumstances and walks alongside us through them. Like Jeremiah, refocusing on Jesus may be what we need.

———————

The reign of Zedekiah was now entrenched in the direction it would go. The king didn't want to listen to Jeremiah; however, Jeremiah had given him and the people a clear message. Destruction was coming if they continued in their present state. God had steadied Jeremiah with a glimpse of the Messiah, so he was ready for the coming clash.

By the third year of Zedekiah's reign, Jeremiah had given the king the message that if he wanted to avoid disaster for the kingdom, he needed to submit to Nebuchadnezzar. The penalty for the sins of Zedekiah and the people was subjugation to Babylon, but it didn't need to get any worse. They could still leave the basket of rotten figs they were in and find mercy. The king, however, didn't want to hear this. He surrounded himself with false prophets who told him that he didn't need to continue in servitude to Babylon. He rejected Jeremiah's message, so Jeremiah preached directly to the priests and the people (Jeremiah 27:12–15), bypassing the king.

Again, Jeremiah told the same message. He told them not to listen to the false prophets, who continued to tell everyone that within two years the exiles would be back from Babylon, bringing with them the gold utensils Nebuchadnezzar had taken from the temple. Jeremiah contested that the prophets were lying to them. He said that if they were true prophets, they would be praying that Nebuchadnezzar didn't return to take the bronze items he had left in the temple. He warned the people that even though God was offering mercy, if the people persisted in rebellion, the end would be death. But they would not listen any more than Zedekiah had (Jeremiah 27:16–22).

Shortly after this, Zedekiah called for a council to be taken with the surrounding nations—Edom, Moab, Ammon, Tyre, and Sidon. With Egypt cowering behind their borders, Zedekiah was still the strongest king in the region. These countries sent envoys to Jerusalem to discuss whether they would be able to band together once again and try to defeat Babylon. Although they had lost their armies just four years earlier, they'd been training a new generation of soldiers and hoped that if they could show Pharaoh their solidarity and strength, Egypt might be persuaded to shake off their fear and join the battle.

As these talks commenced, God spoke to Jeremiah again. This time, Jeremiah was to act out the current situation. Just like a farm animal could be controlled by a yoke and made to work, Nebuchadnezzar had taken control of the entire region. But if they would submit to the yoke of Babylon, they would be allowed to live and remain in their lands. However, if they rebelled, then Nebuchadnezzar would destroy them and take captive those who remained. To help the ambassadors visualize this message, God told Jeremiah to make a yoke and wear it around his neck as he spoke (Jeremiah 27:1–3).

This time, the message was not for Zedekiah, the priests, or the people of Judah. Although Jeremiah was a prophet to Judah, he was also a prophet to the surrounding nations, and he had given many messages to the other nations during his ministry. Jeremiah had already proclaimed this message to Judah, and now he was giving the steps of peace to the surrounding nations. As Zedekiah presided over the talks, Jeremiah walked in, wearing his yoke. After the stir he caused settled down, Jeremiah gave his message to them all. Yahweh, the God of Israel, was also the God of the whole earth. He had made all peoples, and He would determine who ruled over them. For the next three generations, God would give the Babylonian Empire control of all their countries. If they wanted to live, they needed to submit; if they would not bow their neck under his yoke, God would allow Nebuchadnezzar to kill them with the sword, and He would send famine and plague. They were warned not to believe their prophets either, but to trust that the word Jeremiah was speaking was true (Jeremiah 27:4–11).

God's mercy is for all people, and He has shown everyone the pathway of eternal life. We are required to share what we know of God's love with those who are outside of the church as much as we're to help those who are inside. This was a showdown with false prophets for the salvation of pagan nations. All the kings in the region had surrounded themselves with prophets who were telling them that they would be able to throw off the yoke of Babylon and be free again. Jeremiah addressed the gathered ambassadors and called out their prophets as liars. He told them that Yahweh, the God of Israel, was directing history, not Marduk,[4] the god of Babylon, or any of the other gods from the nations represented around the table. Nebuchadnezzar had been given authority by Yahweh, and submitting to Nebuchadnezzar meant submitting to God. In this message, Jeremiah returned to his common pattern in his preaching. He held out a narrow path of mercy while he warned of the wide road of destruction.

In difficult times, it's important to know that God is still in charge, even if evil rulers think they have won. Like Nebuchadnezzar, they are unwittingly God's servants. They have control only for as long as God allows, and the dark times will pass. Even if our nation's ruler is opposed to God and righteousness, that doesn't mean that God was caught off-guard when they were elected. God is still in control. Even in the worst situations, there is always a path of mercy extended to the world. As God's people, we're to ensure that we're on that path and offer it to others.

It had been easy enough for Zedekiah to ignore Jeremiah's message when it had been brought to him privately, but now Zedekiah had

4   Also called Bel, which meant "Master."

been embarrassed in front of ambassadors from five nations with whom he was trying to build an alliance. He knew he couldn't confront the prophet directly, as it would send the wrong message. It was better to let prophets deal with prophets, at least in front of foreign dignitaries. Over the next few days, Zedekiah arranged for the false prophet Hananiah to confront Jeremiah at the temple, where Jeremiah had again been allowed to go. He needed to discredit Jeremiah without turning him into a martyr.

Hananiah cornered Jeremiah and told him that God had a message for Jeremiah. Within two years, the yoke of Babylon would be broken, the people would return along with the gold from the temple and the exiled king, Jehoiachin. Jeremiah longed to believe this message, but it contradicted what God had told him. He told Hananiah that it's easy to prophesy about wars, as there was usually something happening that could be construed to demonstrate that the prophecy had been fulfilled. But when a prophet foretold peace, it would soon be clear if it had come to pass or not. Hananiah replied by doubling down on his word. He came up to Jeremiah and removed the yoke he was wearing and broke it, telling all the people that God would break the yoke of Babylon off the necks of all the nations in two years' time. The theatrics had been beautifully enacted in front of the people, but the intended audience had been the foreign dignitaries. With another prophet discrediting Jeremiah, they could go back to their war council with Zedekiah. Prophecies were used to guide actions. If the yoke of Babylon was to be broken in two years, it would be done by them banding their armies together for war.

Jeremiah left feeling defeated, knowing they were that much closer to a disastrous rebellion. God, however, sent him back with a message for Hananiah and the people. Jeremiah told him that he had only broken a wooden yoke, but God would replace it with an iron one. Because Hananiah had convinced the nations to believe his lies, they would be destroyed. But first, God would destroy Hananiah as a sign to the nations. Hananiah's death would be their warning that they had believed a lie and needed to quickly change course. In less than two months, Hananiah was dead. Unfortunately, the plans for the uprising were not.

Word of Jeremiah's prophecies made it back to Nebuchadnezzar, and he was increasingly pleased with Jeremiah. But word of possible rebellion also came back to the King of Babylon, and he planned how to deal with Zedekiah, the ringleader of a potential rebellion.

Zedekiah was summoned to Babylon to explain himself to Nebuchadnezzar, and Jeremiah took advantage of the event to send another message to the exiles there. He had a word from God about the judgement that would come to Babylon at the end of the seventy years (Jeremiah 51:1–58), so he sent the letter with an officer that was in the entourage. When he got to Babylon, he was to read it to the exiles and then tie it to a rock and throw it into the Euphrates River. Just as it would sink in the river, so too would the Babylonian Empire sink into history (Jeremiah 51:59–64). This was a message from God to assure the exiles that justice would be done, but not through revolt. It would only come about through God's power. No doubt Nebuchadnezzar was informed of this message too, but since it concerned what to him was the distant future, it wasn't a threat, so he ignored it.

When we've been wronged, it's natural to want justice. However, we need to be patient as we wait for God's justice and remember that His timing is not up to us. Very few of the exiles would live to see the fall of Babylon, but they were to trust that God would fulfill His promises.

Meanwhile, Zedekiah managed to convince Nebuchadnezzar that the rumours of rebellion were either not true or that he had seen the sense in not pursuing it and would get the rest of the region to stand down; however he managed it, Zedekiah got himself sent back to Jerusalem, still as king.

Chapter Seven

A CITY UNDER SIEGE

Nebuchadnezzar had delayed Zedekiah's dreams of victory, but they were not abandoned. It took a few more years for the plans that had been set in motion to reach their conclusion and the rebellion to begin. During this time, Ezekiel's prophetic ministry expanded. He was living among the exiles, and he lay siege to a map of Jerusalem in his home. He also had visions of the glory of the Lord departing from the temple (Ezekiel 4:1–17, 10:1–22). God was confirming the message of Jeremiah to the exiles through Ezekiel so that they would submit and turn back to Him in Babylon. This would prepare the next generations for their eventual return.

As the rebellion started, Nebuchadnezzar returned to Jerusalem for a fourth time. This time, he was in no mood to show mercy. Zedekiah locked the city gate, and the city was under siege again. Zedekiah had tried to coordinate a defence with his allies, but against the force of Babylon, they all gave up and Judah was alone when the battle came. Still, the king hoped that Egypt would come to his aid before he would be forced to surrender.

Jeremiah was also in the city, but this time he didn't have any new messages for the king or his people. God was silent as the siege wore on. Egypt didn't arrive, and the people grew desperate. The food started to run out. The people became weak and diseases began to spread. It appeared hopeless, and the king feared the worst. In his despair, he decided that all slaves in the city should be set free. He reasoned that since they would all soon be dead or captured, it was only right that the slaves would be able to face their end as freemen. Zedekiah got all the slave owners in Jerusalem to make a covenant to release their slaves (Jeremiah 34:8–10).

The Law of Moses contained several provisions to take care of the poor, including gleaning rules that forbade farmers from harvesting to the edges of their fields or from making a second pass over them. Once the farmers had done their first pass of the harvest, the poor were to be allowed to come in and take whatever was left behind (Deuteronomy 24:19–21; Leviticus 19:9). Each town was also supposed to have a "food bank" that was supplied every three years by a portion of the harvest gathered as a tax to the food bank. This was to be placed in store for the poor in every city and town (Deuteronomy 14:28–29). As well, every seven years, anyone who owed any debts would have them forgiven. The people were specifically commanded to be generous in loaning the poor what they needed. This was true even if it was close to the seventh year, when the chance of the loan ever being repaid before it was forgiven was very small. And all loans were to be given interest free (Exodus 22:25; Leviticus 25:35–37; Deuteronomy 15:7–11). There were other provisions as well, and all together the rules set up by the Law to care for the poor were very generous.

Even the best social safety nets can fail, and sometimes people would end up under crushing debt and not be able to care for themselves or their families. In those cases, the Law allowed for people to sell themselves into indentured servitude for six years. In exchange for six years of complete service, the buyer would agree to pay off all the person's debts and provide room, board, and clothing for them and their family. This was short-term slavery for the person and their family, but they were to be well cared for and they would also effectively get six years of business training. When the six years were up, they were not to be sent away empty handed, but they were to be provided with livestock, grain, wine, and oil (Exodus 21:2; Deuteronomy 15:12–14). After the six years, the slave would be more than ready to successfully re-enter the work force. If it was done the way it was intended, the slave owner might well come out of the six years worse off financially than if they had just hired a paid worker, but the relationship they built and the support they had been able to give were deemed to be worth more than the expense.

Our attitude toward those in need should always be one of generosity. We should give without expecting anything back. Some people will never be able to take care of all their needs without help, and the church should be first in line to give to them and support them in achieving the most self-reliance they can. This may mean helping them learn life skills that will allow them to succeed, or it may mean providing low income housing, as some churches have done. We can meet the needs any number of ways, first of those in the church but also in our communities. Whatever we do, God is clear that we should be open-handed toward others.

In Jerusalem, as the siege was nearing a year in length, there were plenty of long-term slaves. Along with the usual number of slaves, the wars over the past twenty years had impoverished many people to the point where they were hard-pressed to feed themselves. This had left them desperate and ready to sell themselves into the burgeoning ranks of slavery. However, the people did not obey the Law. There was no generously gifted release given after six years. The slaves were given barely enough to survive, and they were worked hard with no hope of ever being released. Society also failed to maintain the prescribed help for the poor. There were no food banks or fields for gleaning. If people needed a loan, they were offered the option of starving or joining the slave class. Things had gone terribly wrong in Judah. They had been restored under Josiah, but even he hadn't been able to stop all the abuse let alone legislate generosity. Since his death, it had gotten far worse than before (Jeremiah 2:34, 5:28, 22:16).

Given the situation with the siege, one could hardly consider King Zedekiah's act to be a sign of deep repentance, but it was the right thing to do. God is always watching over us for our good, and He will use anything we have that is worthy or true to build us up. Just as God will take the small things in our lives and use them for far greater things in His kingdom, so was His response to Zedekiah. As soon as the people released their slaves as they had been required to do under the

Law, God moved in the heart of Pharaoh, and Egypt started to mobilize its armies. Shortly after that, the news reached Nebuchadnezzar, and he withdrew from the siege of Jerusalem to face off with the attacking army. He wanted to meet them as close as he could to the Egyptian border and drive them back home (Jeremiah 37:5).

This could have been the start of renewal and hope, a time to celebrate, but the people didn't see that God's hand was at work to save them because they had freed the slaves; rather, they saw the fickle hand of fate robbing them of their slaves. Had they known that Egypt was on the way to save them, they would never have released their slaves in the first place! Some of them had only released the slaves so that they wouldn't be required to give them any more food. Now that it appeared Egypt would save them, they immediately broke their covenant and forced their freed slaves back into servitude. Ironically, because of their belief that Pharaoh would save them, they acted just as his predecessor had with Moses, promising to release the people and then chasing them to the Red Sea to force them back into slavery (Jeremiah 34:11). It's amazing that Zedekiah didn't see that he was doing the same thing, or if he did, that he didn't think God would destroy him for the same sins.

After the siege had been lifted and the slaves retaken, Zedekiah sent word to Jeremiah to see if God was finally going to defeat Nebuchadnezzar for them. Even though Zedekiah never allowed himself to be swayed by Jeremiah's advice, he nevertheless wanted to hear it. He'd known from his childhood that Jeremiah was an upright man who loved his nation and its people, but he struggled to understand Jeremiah's faith.

Jeremiah came back with the word that God had given him. Egypt would fail. Nebuchadnezzar would return. Jerusalem would be burned (Jeremiah 37:6–10). Moreover, there would be no relief from the disaster due to the abuse of the slaves. Because they were forced into servitude again after they had been freed, God had decided to "free" the people from life itself. They would die by the sword, plague, and famine (Jeremiah 34:12–22).

Jeremiah isn't recorded as having done any preaching during this siege, but he made up for it after Nebuchadnezzar had withdrawn to fight Egypt. His announcement that their sins would bring back the Babylonians to finish the job they had started made Jeremiah particularly unpopular, but he was still free to come and go as he pleased.

Due to the continuing depopulation of the land through death and desertion, there were a lot of unowned fields. The land was understood to be a sign of God's blessing, and it belonged to the people rather than the state. Unclaimed land was to be given to the people for free, and the only part the government played in the process was to ensure that the partitioning of the land was done fairly. After so many families had fled or been killed, the unowned land needed to be redistributed to the survivors. With Babylon threatening them, this was more hopeful than practical, but they were following the tradition of not allowing the land to remain unclaimed. Jeremiah's home town of Anathoth announced that they were going to allocate the empty land by drawing lots with anyone who was there, so Jeremiah made ready to go home to get his share (Jeremiah 37:11–12).

The land in the Old Testament was a symbol of heaven. It was the eternal possession of the people of God. God had promised to give Abraham land and descendants, so the land was for the families that came from Abraham. As such, it was tied to them just as much as their children were. Even though Jeremiah had been shown by God that the land would be deserted, he also had been given hope that God would not destroy His people altogether. It was an extension of his faith in God to go and receive his share, or "portion," of God's inheritance. Besides, he had been told that he couldn't marry or have children, so the blessing of land seemed to be all that was left for him.

As Jeremiah tried to leave Jerusalem, a guard stopped him and accused him of treason and desertion. The guard assumed he was leaving the city to go over to the Babylonians. After hearing Jeremiah say that the Babylonians would return to destroy the city, it made sense to him that Jeremiah was in league with them rather than that he was a patriotic citizen going to get his portion of the land. At the very least, the guard thought he must be deserting before the next attack. Despite Jeremiah's protestations, he was taken without trial, beaten, and thrown into a dungeon.

Zedekiah knew that Jeremiah had been arrested, but he too was fed up with the prophet and did nothing to rescue him. Zedekiah decided to wait and see if what Jeremiah had foretold would actually come to pass. Perhaps he would call on Jeremiah if he needed another word from the Lord, but only if Nebuchadnezzar did return and lay siege to the city again (Jeremiah 37:13–16).

This unjust imprisonment robbed Jeremiah of his inheritance in the land, since it barred him from going to Anathoth to receive it. God had forbidden him from having an inheritance of children, and now He had allowed Jeremiah to be prevented from receiving an inheritance of land. He must have wondered why God would deny him both blessings. While he lay alone in the dungeon, trying not to move because of the pain of the beating, he sought answers from God, and he questioned if he would even survive. But despite all that he'd been through, and the disaster that was coming, Jeremiah remained convinced that he was still living in God's love.

The word "portion" in the Bible is used as a term of inheritance. The inheritance laws are important for understanding why this was so hard for Jeremiah. When the father passed away, his wealth was divided into even parts, equal to one more than the number of his sons. If there were three sons, then the estate would be divided into four portions. The eldest son, as the principle inheritor for the family, would receive a double portion. The inheritance was for the good of the entire family, and the inheritor was to take care of everyone and manage the estate in trust for their descendants, who would get it in turn. The focus was on the continuity of the family line. This was why a younger brother was sometimes required to marry his brother's widow and give her a son.

This arrangement seems odd and even wrong to us, but we need to understand it in context. If the eldest brother was married but died without an heir, then to maintain the primary family line, the next brother was to give her an heir. We see this with the three brothers

Er, Onan, and Shelah in Genesis. Er would have inherited the double portion, or 50 per cent of his father's estate, whereas Onan and Shelah were in line for only 25 per cent each. When Er died without an heir, that left only two sons, so Onan was in line to inherit the double portion, which would then be 66 per cent of the estate, whereas Shelah would get 33 per cent. However, Onan was supposed to give Er's widow a son. If he had done that, the son would be counted as Er's heir and would have gotten the double portion instead of Onan. That would again have dropped Onan from 66 per cent (or two out of three portions) back to 25 per cent (one out of four portions), which is why he didn't want to get Er's widow pregnant (Genesis 38:8–9).

Had he given his deceased brother's widow an heir, Onan would have given her back her place as the matriarch of the family. This was a practical structure in their society, but it was also intended as a picture of our enduring inheritance with God in heaven.

While in the dungeon, Jeremiah wondered why he not only missed out on receiving the figurative double portion, like the prophet Elisha had received (2 Kings 2:9), but he didn't even get a single portion, because he got neither children nor land. To have no portion at all meant that one was cursed and outcast from God, because he no longer shared in the blessings of the people of God. I believe it was in this crisis of soul that Yahweh spoke to Jeremiah.

Two years later, Jeremiah would write that all which he had hoped for from the Lord was gone (Lamentations 3:18). But immediately after that, he would say that Yahweh was his portion, and he would wait on Him (Lamentations 3:24). I believe that in the dungeon, when all hope of a legacy was gone, Jeremiah learned the depth of God's love for him. God Himself is our portion or inheritance! The land was a shadow of the reality of Jesus, who is our inheritance. Jeremiah was again given a glimpse of the blessing that the cross of Christ would bring.

With each day since Josiah's death, the foretold disaster came closer, and each time the people spurned Yahweh's mercy, the consequences became more severe. By the time Zedekiah had inherited the kingdom, it was a shadow of what his father had ruled over. By the end of this siege, it was only a shadow of what Zedekiah himself had started with. But still there remained an opportunity for redemption, and Jeremiah continued to hope that Zedekiah would grow desperate enough to reach out his hand to God.

How do we respond when it seems like God has denied us His blessing? God doesn't get offended when we question our circumstances, but He wants to lead us to a place of trust, if we let Him. Jeremiah didn't get any quick answers while he sat in jail waiting on the Lord, but through the trial, he slowly learned that what was truly important was his relationship with the eternal God. This enabled him to have hope for his nation.

We need to see our world through God's eyes. He is at work in our lives and in our nation, even if we don't always see it. We must wait on Him for ourselves and maintain hope for those we love who, like Zedekiah, may be living in opposition to God. We must remain faithful to pray for them, because giving up is easy. We may be tempted to think that God doesn't care about the people or situations we pray for because we don't see any changes, but God is more concerned than we are. Just as God loved Jeremiah and placed him where he was as a witness, so too He loves us and has placed us where we can be a witness to those around us. Out of His boundless love, He has given us Himself as our portion and inheritance.

Chapter Eight

THE DESTROYER

While Jeremiah suffered in the dungeon, Nebuchadnezzar defeated Pharaoh and sent him back across his borders, where he would stay. Then Nebuchadnezzar turned his eye back to Jerusalem and started the siege all over. The previous time, Babylon had needed to split its army so they could also attack other nations in the region. This time, the entire army was focused on Judah (2 Kings 25:1; Jeremiah 39:1, 52:4–5).

After the siege had settled in, Zedekiah decided to ask Jeremiah if God was willing to rescue them with a miracle, like He had in the past. The false prophets with whom he surrounded himself were willing to tell the king what he wanted to hear, but he knew that Jeremiah wouldn't hold back the truth. Still, Zedekiah wasn't sure if he believed what Jeremiah had to say or not. He was just hedging his bets; nevertheless, he sent a messenger to ask Jeremiah to inquire of God (Jeremiah 21:1–2).

The word Jeremiah had for the king was not what he wanted to hear. Not only would Nebuchadnezzar win, but God would be fighting on the enemy's side. The people inside the city would either starve to death, die of disease, or be killed by the attacking army.

By this time, Jeremiah had been foretelling the destruction of Judah for more than forty years, so this wasn't unexpected. But there had always been hope if the people repented. God no longer offered this hope. The nation would not survive; however, God still gave the people a way out.

Jeremiah told the king that if he wanted to save the people, they needed to surrender. Anyone who went out to Nebuchadnezzar and surrendered would live, but death awaited those who stayed in the city.

God had promised Baruch the hope of escaping with his life, and now He offered it to anyone who would submit to Babylon. Next, Jeremiah explained to the king that he was responsible to administer justice, but because he was not doing so, God was justified in His anger (Jeremiah 21:3–14).

People complain that the God of the Old Testament is a God of judgement, but then the same people complain that God allows evil in the world. We can't have it both ways. To rid the world of evil, God must judge evil people. King Zedekiah was wicked. He perverted justice in the courts, as did the rest of his officials, and the people also followed the king in this. Jeremiah was a witness to the justice of God, but at every turn, God also held out mercy. Even in this last siege, anyone could surrender to Babylon and live.

Our times aren't much different than Jeremiah's. We are a nation that has turned away from God and turned against each other. Even so, God's mercy is extended to us. A day will come when His judgement will right all wrongs, but praise God that for now His love is holding back judgement so that everyone may repent and surrender to Jesus.

Zedekiah had not gone in person to Jeremiah, nor had he brought Jeremiah to the palace. He had just sent a messenger to see what Jeremiah would say. Now he wondered if Jeremiah felt slighted and wasn't willing to ask God to help. The king believed that the gods were powerful but fickle and that they could be manipulated with the right ceremonies, prayers, and gifts, so he decided to try again and had Jeremiah brought to him this time.

When Jeremiah arrived at the palace, he was ushered into a private audience with the king. Zedekiah asked him again if there was a new word from the Lord. Jeremiah repeated that he would be delivered to the king of Babylon, but this time he also pleaded his own wrongful imprisonment to the king. As proof of his innocence, he reminded the king that the false prophets had been proven wrong, whereas he had been proven right; therefore, it wasn't fair to imprison him for telling the truth in Yahweh's name. He petitioned the king to not send him back to die in the dungeon.

Zedekiah agreed and had him held at the courtyard of the guard instead. He made sure that Jeremiah got bread every day until the city ran out of food altogether. He wasn't prepared to set Jeremiah free, because he wasn't happy with the message that he must surrender or die in Babylon, but he compromised by giving him better conditions (Jeremiah 37:17–21, 32:1–5).

Jeremiah's imprisonment seemed harsh, but it was part of God's plan. Because Jeremiah had been in the dungeon almost since the end of the previous siege, he couldn't be blamed for the return of the Babylonian army. God had protected him and was fulfilling His promise to keep Jeremiah safe. He wasn't where he wanted to be, but he was where God wanted him to be. We may not understand why God allows hardship in our lives, but we need to trust that His love and protection never fails.

While Jeremiah was living as a detainee in the courtyard of the guard, God spoke to him. He told Jeremiah that his cousin was going to come to him and offer to sell him some property. Very likely, his cousin had just been allocated the land for free at the same land redistribution that Jeremiah had tried to attend. Then, as the food got scarce in Jerusalem, his cousin decided to sell it so that he'd have money to buy bread. Since they were of the same family, the land title could be permanently sold as opposed to just being leased, since by law land wasn't to be transferred between different families (Leviticus 25:14–16). God revealed to Jeremiah that he was to buy the land as a sign to the people that, one day, Judah would be restored as a country and they would again be able to buy and sell land.

Later that day, his cousin arrived with the proposal, and Jeremiah agreed and bought the land in front of witnesses. Baruch, Jeremiah's friend and scribe, wrote up the purchase deed. Then, as was the custom, he wrote two copies of the contract; one was sealed and the other was left open. The open copy was for anyone to read; however, because it could be tampered with, a sealed copy was created. Should there be any question about the legitimacy of the open copy, the sealed copy could be opened in front of witnesses to confirm the details of the transaction. Jeremiah had both copies placed in a clay jar so that they would last a long time, and then he told the people that this was a sign that God would bring them back one day and make the country vibrant again (Jeremiah 32:6–16).

We too have both a sealed and open contract with God through Jesus Christ. His promise to us is heaven, and the seal of the promise is the Holy Spirit (Ephesians 1:13). Our testimony serves as the open contract for the world to read, but of course it can be altered or faked. We have all seen leaders in the church who later deny their faith, or we know of people who claim to be Christians, but their lives seem to deny the truth of their words. We're not their judge, but one day the sealed copy will be opened in the courts of heaven for all to see, and God will reveal the truth.

We can be religious without having a relationship with God. We can go to church. We can give a tithe. We can volunteer and live a good life. Those are all good things, but they should result from a true relationship with God, not merely an adherence to the rules we think we must obey. Only through coming to Jesus, who has purchased our forgiveness with His blood (Revelation 5:9), can we know that our name is written on the sealed contract (Revelation 13:8).

Once the contract was complete, Jeremiah went back to a private place and asked God about it. He prayed a long and eloquent prayer, recounting all of God's miracles on behalf of His people, and then he ended with the obvious. Babylon was at the gate, and the message of mercy no longer included any chance of the people remaining in the land—only having their lives spared. What good was the land now? Jeremiah's prayer could easily be summarized in a single word: seriously? God lovingly responded. He told Jeremiah that he was right. The city would be burned and the land taken because of the sins of the people. They worshipped false gods and sacrificed their children to them, but Jeremiah was looking only at the immediate future. In God's mind, the future was bright. The people would return, and He would make an enduring covenant with them. He wouldn't leave their inheritance as a desolate wasteland but would restore their fortunes (Jeremiah 32:17–44).

This was why Jeremiah had been prevented from getting the land for free. It was far more powerful for him to purchase it and show the people that there was hope. There was good reason to surrender to Nebuchadnezzar, because they could still live, and the surrender wouldn't be the end. The King of Babylon was just for the moment, but God's promises were forever. Jeremiah's land purchase affirmed the fact that God still extended His mercy to the people.

We live in a world of fear, especially for the younger generation. They are taught to fear environmental change, people from the other side of the political spectrum, big business and the rich, other races, and in some cases their own race. Society is turning against Christians, and we wonder what will happen next, or if we should even bring children into this world.

I was initially attracted to the story of Jeremiah because of the similarities to our culture and the fear that our nation is moving quickly toward judgement. Maybe it is, but I was wrong to look at the future with apprehension. In this simple land purchase, we see that God doesn't intend for us to live in fear. He's in control of today and is planning a brighter tomorrow. Eventually, judgement will come to everyone who rejects Jesus, but we don't need to be afraid when we trust in Him.

God's plans are far too complex for us to second guess. In all that Jeremiah had gone through, God had been guiding the circumstances for His glory. Just as Jeremiah was continually learning to trust, so we must trust God. Even when it seems that our lives are upside down, if we are submitting to Him, He will work all things for our good (Romans 8:28).

———

As Jeremiah reflected on what God had told him about the land, God also spoke to him about restoration. God confirmed that the houses of

Jerusalem would soon be filled with the dead, but He immediately gave Jeremiah a vision of the time of renewal. Like the dream Jeremiah had had a few years earlier, this vision didn't just focus on the return in seventy years, but it looked forward to the Messiah. He spoke about the righteous branch that would sprout from David's line, which looked forward to Jesus, whose love endures forever (Jeremiah 33:1–26).

Jeremiah saw how the rulers of the people were destroying the nation with their lies about God, but the Messiah would establish truth (Jeremiah 23:1–8). As Jeremiah considered the contrast between the deceptive prophets who had led the people to the desperate state they were in, and the righteous Saviour who would come, he began to comprehend the broken heart of God for His people. Jeremiah wept for the loss of so many lives. The job of a prophet was to turn the people from evil deeds, but these false prophets had encouraged all manner of wickedness. They fabricated messages from Yahweh just to support their own evil actions. In contrast, God's Word was powerful and ignited passion in the hearts of those who would hear it (Jeremiah 23:9–40).

When we meditate on God, He often leads us to compassion for the lost. This was true for Jeremiah, who saw God's eternal plan for their salvation. He came to understand that it was not God's desire to punish, but it was man's depravity that demands judgement. We must never look at people as objects of God's wrath; instead, we need to see through the broken heart of God's love.

———

Jeremiah was refreshed by the vision of God's salvation, and it compelled him to share God's message to see the people spared. This meant that he passionately tried to persuade the people to surrender. At that time, Jeremiah was still in the courtyard of the guard, so most of the people he preached to were young soldiers, and he was counselling them to desert! He told the same thing to anyone else who passed by. As a result, the officials were furious with him. They went to the king to get Zedekiah to execute Jeremiah. The king was losing his hold over the people, and he was afraid of his officials, so he told them to do whatever they believed right, and he wouldn't interfere. This wasn't exactly what they'd hoped for, as they were a little superstitious about killing a prophet. But when they left the king, they had Jeremiah thrown into a dry cistern. At the bottom was a few feet of mud, and they reasoned that Jeremiah would die in the cistern without them having to physically kill him. If he got too weak to stand, he would slip under the mud and suffocate. If he managed to avoid that somehow, he would starve to death (Jeremiah 38:1–6).

But even in this, God was protecting Jeremiah. Ebed-Melek, a Cushite official at the palace, saw what had happened and went to King Zedekiah to apprise him of the situation. Since Jeremiah was still alive, Zedekiah decided to send Ebed-Melek to rescue him. He was pulled out of the pit and placed back in the court of the guard, where he lived until the city was taken (Jeremiah 38:7–13).

As Jeremiah was recovering from this latest ordeal, he had a word from God for his rescuer. God would destroy the city, but Ebed-Melek would be saved out of it because he trusted God and rescued Jeremiah, even though doing so had placed him at risk (Jeremiah 39:15–18). God was still finding and protecting His remnant. Even when things look bleak, God is at work, leaving the ninety-nine to seek for the one (Matthew 18:12). We can be assured that God is watching over each of us.

Zedekiah then sent for Jeremiah again and met him in secret by the temple. He asked Jeremiah what God was revealing to the prophet and told him to answer honestly, holding nothing back. Jeremiah was skeptical and told Zedekiah that if he did, the king would just kill him or, at best, not listen. Zedekiah swore that he wouldn't kill him or hand him over again to those who wanted him dead.

Jeremiah told the king again that if he surrendered, he and his family would live, and the city would survive too. This was the first time since the last siege had begun that God offered to spare the city and not just the lives of the people who surrendered. As king, Zedekiah held the future of the nation in his hands. God even assured the king through Jeremiah that he would be protected from anyone who might think he was a traitor for not having held out. If he didn't surrender, he would be captured. Just as Jeremiah had been physically sunk in the mud that might have suffocated him, the king would be sunk in spiritual mud that would destroy him.

The king was still afraid of the people. He didn't want anyone to know that he had talked to the prophet, so he swore Jeremiah to secrecy and sent him back to the courtyard of the guard (Jeremiah 38:14–28).

Jeremiah often used the phrase/., "terror on every side." King Zedekiah feared the future and couldn't settle on a course of action, because all options could turn out badly. In his mind, there was terror whichever way he turned. When we fail to trust God for the future, it can appear like there's terror on every side. But when we are immersed in the love of God, we no longer need to fear anything. Perfect love casts out fear (1 John 4:18), and we can rest in the knowledge that even though we don't know the future, we're in the hands of a God who does.

As the siege wore down to the final months and days, the people in the city ran out of food. Many of the women who were pregnant miscarried due to their poor health, and when they did, they hid themselves so that they could eat their stillborn babies and not have to share them with their families. This was the final extreme they were driven to. It was God's way of demonstrating for all time how precious children are. Yes, it was horrible, but after generations of sacrificing their children to Moloch and not listening to the prophets who told them how evil that was, God forced them to participate in their depravity first-hand (Jeremiah 19:9; Lamentations 2:20). The horror that they must have felt as they ate their own children was only a fraction of what God had felt with each child that had been burned alive in their demonic worship.

People in our society might claim that this demonstrates the Old Testament God to be heartless, while they ironically defend abortion. This story is horrendous, but it shows God bringing justice to the unborn. Jeremiah didn't judge these desperate people who thought there was no other way out of their circumstances. He was placed by God to offer mercy, forgiveness, and healing to the parents. God still wants to heal those who have been caught in our world's lies and have decided for abortion. This is a shocking story to get our attention, but it's intended to lead to repentance and restoration, not condemnation. There is healing for our souls at the cross!

The end was bitter hard, but just before it came, Jeremiah was given a final word for the king, whom he had helped to raise. Nebuchadnezzar would shortly break through the walls and burn down the city. He would capture the king, but he wouldn't kill him. Zedekiah would die peacefully and be mourned by his people (Jeremiah 34:1–7).

It can be hard to understand why people we view as deserving of judgement receive any mercy at all. Zedekiah had watched his brother's body decay outside the city walls, and God was letting him know that he would not be dishonoured in that way. Perhaps the lesson for us is that we're not to judge others. Jeremiah could easily have given in to hatred for Zedekiah, but he didn't. He continued to love him and to plead with the people. He held out the mercy of God, which was available until the end.

Finally, when the attacking army broke through the wall, the defenders had no strength left to fight. Nebuchadnezzar's men committed rape, pillage, and slaughter from house to house. In the mayhem that night, the king and his army were spotted sneaking out of the city. In the pursuit that followed, the king was separated from his army and captured. He was then taken to Nebuchadnezzar, who had his sons killed in front of him. We don't know how old his sons were, but Zedekiah was only thirty-two, so they would have been teenagers or younger. Finally, they put his eyes out and took him to Babylon (2 Kings 25:4–7; Jeremiah 39:2–7, 52:7–11).

Meanwhile, back in Jerusalem, all the walls around the city were broken down. The temple, the palace, and all the important buildings and houses were burned. The rest of the treasures from the temple were plundered, and the larger items were broken up for transportation to

Babylon (2 Kings 25:9–10, 13–17; 2 Chronicles 36:18–19; Jeremiah 39:8, 52:12–14, 17–23).

Jeremiah hadn't been killed but he was captured, and he watched the destruction. Only twenty-three years earlier, Judah had been a free state with several million citizens. With the fall of Jerusalem, it was reduced to only a few thousand conquered souls. Two decades of war had seen almost everyone flee or be killed, and the remnant were either already in Babylon or they were in chains, waiting to be deported.

God hadn't placed Jeremiah there just to warn of coming judgement. He was also there as a witness so that there would be a record of the sorrow of God's broken heart. There's nothing more tragic in the Old Testament than the destruction of Jerusalem and what it symbolized. Jesus would weep over the city and say, *"Jerusalem, Jerusalem, you who kill the prophets and stone those sent to you, how often I have longed to gather your children together, as a hen gathers her chicks under her wings, and you were not willing"* (Luke 13:34) This city was meant to be the heart of God's people and a light in a dark and needy world. But they had completely perverted God's revelation so that the world was almost entirely without a witness. *"God ... sent word to them through his messengers again and again, because he had pity on his people..."* (2 Chronicles 36:15). But finally, God's heart broke and He allowed His people to be destroyed. God's sobbing still echoes in Jeremiah's shattered heart for us to hear.

What choice had the people left God? They were guilty of taking advantage of poor widows, orphans, and immigrants. Violent crime was rampant. They took and held slaves. Murder was at an all time high. They forced their children into prostitution and committed incest and child abuse. Adultery and all types of sexual sins gripped the nation, and they practised infanticide. Finally, they had justified their sins by embracing religions that encouraged these practices, and they worshipped these false gods. God had not abandoned His people, but they had completely abandoned Him.

But even in the middle of the most violent attack on the Jewish people since they had been slaves in Egypt, the mercy and love of God was shown again. There were a few in the city who were not killed, and there were more that had listened to Jeremiah and surrendered to the Babylonians. God spared their lives as promised. As even more proof of God's mercy, the poorest of the people, who would have been the slaves released but then forced back into slavery, were left in the land. Nebuchadnezzar wanted to profit from his conquest, but to do that, he needed people to work the land for him. So these slaves, who should have been generously freed by their owners, were generously freed by God instead. They were given vineyards and fields and left to enjoy their lives in the land under Babylon's governor (2 Kings 25:11–12; 2 Chronicles 36:20; Jeremiah 39:9–10, 52:15–16).

God's justice may not come as quickly as we would like, but He will ensure that justice is done. We need to wait on the Lord, because we will see His righteousness displayed. Sometimes grace comes in the rubble of judgement, because until we understand our sins, we cannot embrace our Father's forgiveness. The bad news of our rebellion against God must always precede the good news of His love and the sacrifice that bought our pardon.

Chapter Nine

THE AFTERMATH

When the war was over, Jeremiah was in chains, waiting to be taken into exile with the rest of the captives; however, Nebuchadnezzar had been keeping tabs on Jeremiah since he'd sent his first letter to the captives back in Babylon. Also, the people who had surrendered had told their captors that Jeremiah had been telling everyone to surrender. Because of this, Nebuchadnezzar had given orders not to harm Jeremiah but to let him go and give him whatever he wanted. When he was found among the other captives, he was freed and given provisions and a gift from King Nebuchadnezzar. He was told that he would be well taken care of if he decided to go to Babylon, but if he still wanted to stay in Judah, he was free to go anywhere he pleased. It was suggested that if he stayed, he should go and live with the newly appointed governor, Gedaliah. Jeremiah agreed to go there, and he and Baruch went to stay with the governor. We're not told why Baruch was included, but Jeremiah may have asked for his friend's release as well. Perhaps Baruch's freedom was the gift that Jeremiah had been given (Jeremiah 39:11–14, 40:1–6).

Jeremiah knew the new governor. Gedaliah's father, Ahikam, had saved Jeremiah's life back at the beginning of Jehoiakim's reign more than twenty years earlier (Jeremiah 26:24). The fact that Gedaliah had been chosen to be the governor shows that his family had continued to believe and support the prophet. They accepted the fact that Babylon was being used by God to correct His people, so they submitted to

Nebuchadnezzar. It was natural that Jeremiah would go to live with him and try to rebuild a community among the remnant of the people in Judah.

The slaves that were freed and given land were also settled near the new governor in Mizpah. Soon everyone else who was hiding throughout the country came to Gedaliah. Half a dozen army officers who had escaped with the remains of their regiments now came out of hiding. These would have been from the forces that fled Jerusalem with Zedekiah but had been separated from him. Among them was Ishmael, an officer from the royal family. All the people who came to Gedaliah were settled into abandoned towns and assured they'd be safe, even though there was a garrison from Babylon at Mizpah. If the people paid their taxes and served the King of Babylon, they wouldn't have any further problems (2 Kings 25:22–24; Jeremiah 40:7–10).

As the settlement became established, the Jews that had fled to nearby countries like Moab, Ammon, and Edom heard about the growing community that had been left behind. They too returned, and God gave the group an abundant harvest in the first year they were back. God was comforting His people and reinforcing the governor's words that things would now get better (Jeremiah 40:11–12). However, He would give them another test to see if they were ready to turn back to Yahweh.

Among the army officers who had returned, rumours arose that Ishmael was working with the king of the Ammonites. The other officers came to Gedaliah with their concerns that Ishmael had been sent to assassinate the governor. Presumably, because he was from the royal family, and Gedaliah was not, Ishmael was jealous of Gedaliah's appointment, so he had agreed to work with the Ammonites to undermine the colony that was beginning to stabilize in Judah. Unfortunately, the governor didn't believe their report. He knew Ishmael and didn't believe he would do such a thing, so when one of the officers offered to pre-emptively kill Ishmael, the governor forbade him (Jeremiah 40:13–16).

A short time later, Ishmael was in Mizpah with ten of his men. They were feasting with Gedaliah, who also had several men with him, including the Babylonian soldiers from the garrison. If Gedaliah had any misgivings about Ishmael, they were calmed by the surroundings and the strength of the men with him; however, Ishmael was waiting for the perfect moment when everyone had their guard down. Then, while they were eating, he attacked and killed Gedaliah and everyone with him (2 Kings 25:25; Jeremiah 41:1–3).

Ishmael wasn't safe, however, because there were a lot of people coming and going in Mizpah. Since the temple was destroyed, Jeremiah had moved the centre of worship to Mizpah. He couldn't offer animal sacrifices, but other offerings and prayers could be made. Jeremiah was attempting to train the people in the ways of the Lord. While he was there, he wrote the book of Lamentations to remind the people that their sins had brought about the destruction but also to give them hope that God's compassion is new every morning (Lamentations 3:22–23).

The day after the assassination, eighty men arrived to worship. They were in mourning for the destruction of Jerusalem and were bringing offerings. Ishmael saw them coming and knew they could overpower his handful of men, so he went out to them and deceived them and led them into an ambush. He had seventy of them killed and hid their bodies with the others he had killed the day before, but ten of them traded their lives for some food that they'd hidden nearby (Jeremiah 41:4–9).

It's hard to understand why God would allow these men to be killed as they came to worship; however, they were coming to pray to the false gods that had been allowed in Jerusalem under six of the last seven kings. They had not turned back to Yahweh. They had cut themselves as a sign of their mourning, which Yahweh had forbidden but which was common in the pagan worship. God was still purging the evil ways from His people.

Ishmael hadn't intended to kill the seventy men, but once we start down a path of deception, it takes over our lives, making it hard to regain control. He needed more time to get away, so their arrival forced him to slaughter them as well. Although we hopefully aren't killing people in our lives, we may allow lies to take root, and it requires more deception to cover the first lies until our lives are out of our control.

Ishmael took captive all the people who were there, including the young daughters of King Zedekiah, along with Jeremiah and Baruch. Then he started back to Ammon; however, the rest of the army officers heard about it from their nearby towns, and they mustered the last of the army of Judah and pursued Ishmael. They managed to free all the captives, but Ishmael escaped back to the King of Ammon (Jeremiah 41:10–15).

The people were free from Ishmael, but they were terrified by what they imagined King Nebuchadnezzar would do when he found out that his governor and some of his soldiers had been killed. Would retribution be taken against the Jews rather than the Ammonites? Rather than going back to Mizpah, they decided to flee to Egypt with all the people they had rescued. When they came near Bethlehem, they stopped to rest and turned to Jeremiah for advice. The army officers leading them would have heard Jeremiah preaching while he was being held in the courtyard of the guard in Jerusalem. At that time, he had told them to desert and surrender to Babylon, but they hadn't listened to him. But now they wanted to know what Yahweh would tell them. This was God's test to see if they would finally listen to Him and obey. If they would, then the colony would be allowed to remain, but if not, they'd be destroyed, just as Jerusalem had been. God had already shown them mercy through their bountiful first harvest after the destruction of Jerusalem, so that they would know that He had their restoration at heart (2 Kings 25:26; Jeremiah 41:16–18, 42:1–3).

Jeremiah promised to pray and ask Yahweh for guidance, and the leaders promised that whatever the word from God was, they would obey it. So they camped there and waited while Jeremiah prayed. It was ten days before God gave His prophet the direction they were seeking. When Jeremiah came back to the people, he spoke to everyone and not just the leaders, so that they could each decide if they trusted God enough to obey Him. Baruch stood with him as he again brought a message of hope, mercy, and grace to the people. If they would stay in

Judah, God would bless them. The time for disaster was over, and they could continue to build. This was an opportunity for them to remain in the land and prepare it for the eventual return of those who had gone to Babylon. God would build up His people in both places and then re-unite them when the seventy years of exile was over. They didn't need to fear Nebuchadnezzar, as God would have compassion on them and protect them from the king (Jeremiah 42:4–12).

Sometimes we ask God for help, and He specifically addresses our concerns, but then we doubt Him anyway. If we don't trust and obey, we'll miss the blessings God has for us. The people didn't know God, and they didn't trust Jeremiah. They thought he was just saying what they secretly wanted to hear, but they didn't believe it could be true. They were sure he was making it up to destroy them. We can only learn to know His voice through a consistent relationship with God (John 10:27). These people didn't want to come under the rule of God, so they couldn't hear His voice.

God had shown His prophet that the people would rebel again, so Jeremiah continued with the bad news. If they disobeyed and fled to Egypt to avoid war and famine, then war and famine would follow them there and they would all die in Egypt. By asking God what to do and promising to obey when they really intended to do their own thing, they made themselves guiltier than before they asked. Since they appeared determined to go to Egypt anyway, they would all die there (Jeremiah 42:13–22).

The leaders were indignant. They told Jeremiah that he was lying, and that God really wanted them to go to Egypt. They said that Baruch was directing Jeremiah as to what he should say, because he wanted to see the Babylonians come and kill them or force them into exile in Babylon (Jeremiah 43:1–3). Even though it made little sense for the people to voluntarily exile themselves in Egypt to avoid exile in Babylon, the leaders let their fear have control.

Sometimes we may be afraid that if we follow God, He'll take away all the things we love or want in life, and in turn leave us with only harsh rules. In fact, God wants to give us abundant life, but some of the things we think will give us joy are the very things that prevent us from walking into the good life God has for us. We must not let fear keep us from embracing that life. God may ask us to give up a lucrative job in order to move into ministry. Trust Him to take care of the finances. Other times He may move us out of ministry and into something where we're better positioned to reach others. Trust that it will be rewarding.

All the people who had been left in Judah, along with those who had returned from other countries, refused to stay. They chose to flee again to Egypt. Even the slaves to whom God had given land decided to abandon the blessing of God and showed themselves to be just as disobedient as their former masters. The army officers also forced Jeremiah and Baruch to go with them (Jeremiah 43:4–7), but this too was another move of God to hold out mercy as He sent His prophet with a message for the refugees in Egypt.

Jeremiah would give his final prophecies in Egypt. Most of the people who had left during the battles with the Babylonians had fled to Egypt. Those who had fled to other countries and those who had remained in Judah arrived in Egypt with Jeremiah. Except for a few hundred people, Judah was empty, and all the remaining Jews were living either in Babylon or in Egypt.

When they reached the city of Tahpanhes, the Lord spoke to Jeremiah. Pharaoh had a palace there, and Jeremiah took some large stones and buried them in the clay by the entrance to the palace. He did this while all the Jews were watching, both those who forced him to go to Egypt and the others who had come to Egypt previously. Then he told them that Nebuchadnezzar would soon come there too. He would conquer Pharaoh and would set up his throne on top of the stones that Jeremiah had just buried. When the King of Babylon arrived, he would kill the people there just as he had in Jerusalem. The Jews who had fled for safety would find themselves right back in the situation they had just left. Nebuchadnezzar would burn the city and the temples, just as he'd done in Judah (Jeremiah 43:8–13).

When God disciplines us and teaches us how to follow Him more faithfully, it's good to submit and learn (Lamentations 3:27). For the benefit of our souls, He'll allow us to walk through the same lesson as many times as required for us to learn it. But if we submit the first time, God will teach us before the lessons and the consequences become too severe. We can all think of sins we have struggled with and how they grew stronger in our lives until we finally allowed God to deal with them. At each turn, the consequences were harder. This is the mercy of God, who pulls us to Himself until we give in and are engulfed in His embrace.

Finally, Jeremiah met with the colonies of Jews living in Egypt. They had settled in several cities, so Jeremiah went from place to place to bring them the last message that Yahweh had given him and to plead with them. However, everywhere he went he received the same answer. He reminded them of everything that God had done to correct His people. They had rejected God and burned incense to false gods, who allowed them to indulge all their evil desires. God had sent prophets to call them back to Himself, but they wouldn't listen. Instead, they became worse and worse, so God had punished them. Now Judah and Jerusalem were destroyed completely. The people who had come to Egypt had brought all their false worship with them and were no better than those who had been killed in Judah. If they insisted on continuing to live without regard for Yahweh, then the disaster that had come on Judah would follow them to Egypt. They would die there, and none of them would return to the land God had given them when He chose them to be His people. They could save themselves, but only if they turned back to their God (Jeremiah 44:1–14).

All the people, men and women together, told Jeremiah that they had no intention of turning back from worshipping the Queen of Heaven.[5] The Jews living in Egypt had brought with them the same mixed worship of Yahweh, Asherah, and other gods that Manasseh had encouraged just before Jeremiah's birth. They told Jeremiah that under Manasseh and the early reign of Josiah, things had been wonderful, and

---

5   This was a term used for various sky goddesses, including Asherah.

Asherah had provided for them. In their opinion, things started to go wrong when Josiah began his reforms and angered the goddess. When they reflected on the war and destruction of the past twenty-four years since Josiah's death, they blamed the lack of devotion to Asherah for Jerusalem's destruction and not their faithlessness to Yahweh. They laid the blame at the feet of Jeremiah for preaching against their goddess, and they insisted that their devotion in Egypt would set things right. They all agreed that this was what they intended to do (Jeremiah 44:15–19).

For Jeremiah, this was the ultimate slap in the face. His life's work had been to show people the love and mercy of God and to plead with them to come to Him and live. He hadn't met with much success, although there were some people still alive in Babylon because they had listened. Jeremiah was close to seventy years old and had been preaching to the people for more than forty years. All the destruction that he'd tried to steer the people away from had come to pass, and now they blamed him and his message for it. They still couldn't see that it was because of their sins.

When we look at our lives and try to determine if we have succeeded, we must not judge based on human success. Jeremiah had chronicled the heart of God for His people. He had lived out chapters of his life that foreshadowed the suffering that Christ would one day take on for us, and he had left a message of hope and love that would endure for thousands of years. More than that, he had been faithful to his Lord. But at this moment, he felt like a failure.

Jeremiah told the people that they had it all wrong. It was the false worship of the Queen of Heaven that had brought on them all the punishments of Yahweh. But if they were determined to continue, then they should go ahead and live how they pleased. But they should know that they were bringing on themselves the same punishment. Almost no one from that group or their children would ever return to Judah, and they would be cut off from being the people of God. As proof, Yahweh would soon give them a sign. Pharaoh would be defeated by his enemies (Jeremiah 44:20–30).

God gave mankind free will, and He has never revoked it. Jeremiah knew that if they were determined to turn from God, he couldn't stop them. He could only warn them of the consequences and leave them in God's hands. We must not think that we can force people to see truth or turn to God. We can only pray that they will. Then the rest is between them and God.

We don't know if Jeremiah lived to see Pharaoh defeated or not. This was the last confrontation recorded between him and the rebellious people. Baruch compiled the book of Jeremiah and Lamentations as a collection of vignettes about his life and messages, and then Jeremiah died in Egypt. He had touched the lives of people like Daniel and Ezekiel, and he had persuaded hundreds, or perhaps thousands, to turn back to God. But he had watched as millions would not.

Today, Western culture is just as opposed to God as the Jewish people were during Jeremiah's life. In our time, people believe whatever allows them to live as they please. The poor are exploited or used for political gain, but they're not cared for. We see injustice in our courts and a rise of violent crime and murder. There's as much violence in families and homes as on our streets. Our culture is completely obsessed with pornography and sexual indulgence, and as a result, millions of unwanted babies are aborted. But into this darkness, God is calling His people to be lights of purity, holiness, and forgiveness. He wants to raise an army of Jeremiahs who will extend the love, mercy, and grace of God to our lost generation. Jeremiah's example serves as a powerful testimony of speaking the Word of God fearlessly—both the bad news of sin and judgement and the good news of forgiveness and relationship with God.

We are living in the "now" of God's salvation (2 Corinthians 6:2). Judgement is coming on the world, but now there is still time to reach people for Christ. Now the church needs to be salt and light in a dark and decaying world. Now we must trust that God won't allow His Word to return to Him void but will ensure that it accomplishes everything He has planned (Isaiah 55:11).

THE KINGS OF JEREMIAH

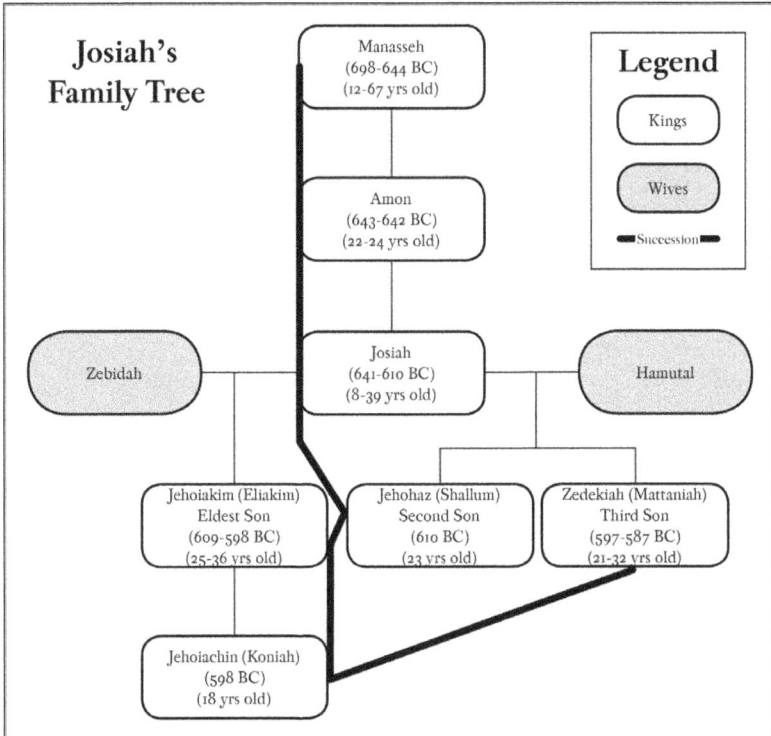

Josiah's Family Tree

Manasseh
(698-644 BC)
(12-67 yrs old)

Amon
(643-642 BC)
(22-24 yrs old)

Zebidah

Josiah
(641-610 BC)
(8-39 yrs old)

Hamutal

Jehoiakim (Eliakim)
Eldest Son
(609-598 BC)
(25-36 yrs old)

Jehoahaz (Shallum)
Second Son
(610 BC)
(23 yrs old)

Zedekiah (Mattaniah)
Third Son
(597-587 BC)
(21-32 yrs old)

Jehoiachin (Koniah)
(598 BC)
(18 yrs old)

Legend

Kings

Wives

Succession

To keep the kings and the timeline straight, centre on Josiah. The story starts with his grandfather and father, then after Josiah it moves on to his three sons, with a brief stop at one of his grandsons.

TIMELINE

The dates on this timeline are pinned to well-known dates and should be accurate to within a year or two. This assumes that Jeremiah was born ten years before the end of Manasseh's reign, although that could be off by a few years. The life of kings is shown by a dotted line until the start of their reign. Josiah's reign is shown in light blue to allow easy reference of who was alive during it.

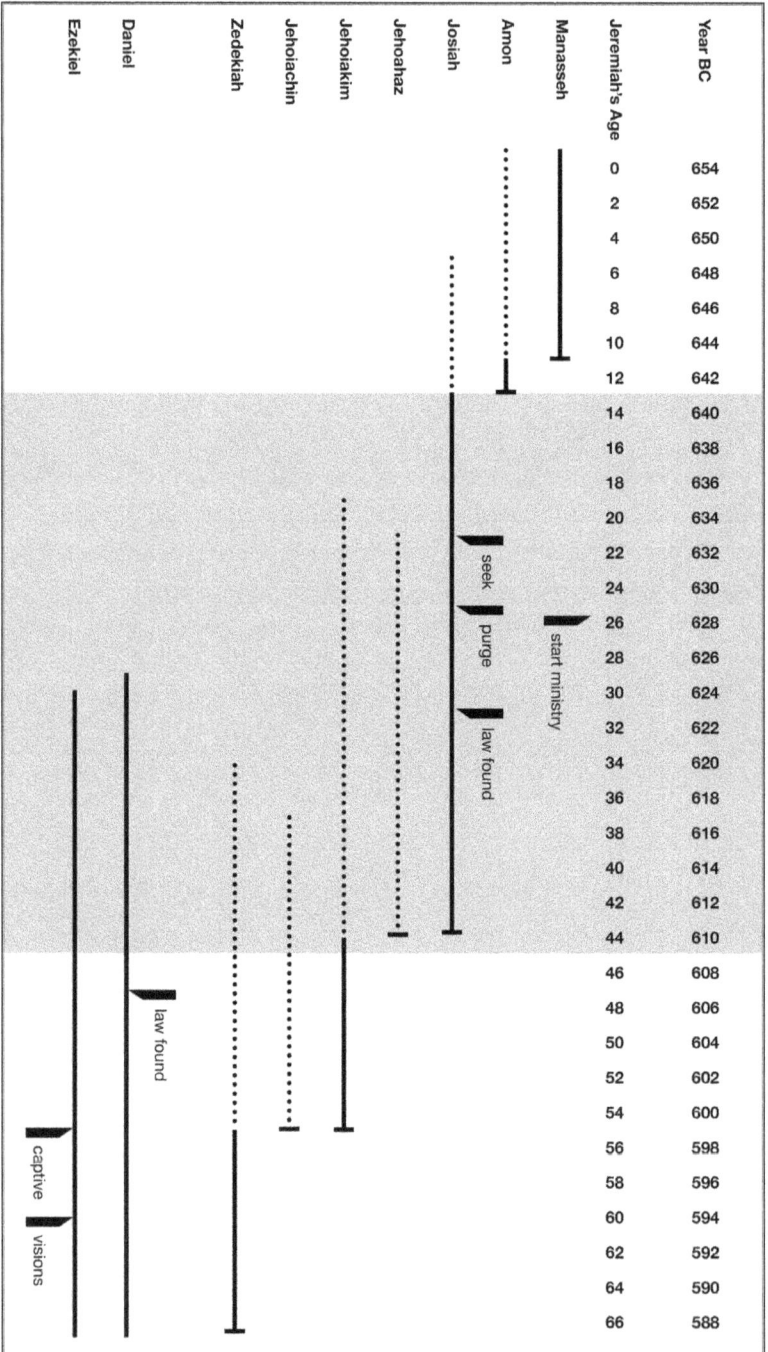

Year BC	Jeremiah's Age	Manasseh	Amon	Josiah	Jehoahaz	Jehoiakim	Jehoiachin	Zedekiah	Daniel	Ezekiel
654	0									
652	2									
650	4									
648	6									
646	8									
644	10									
642	12									
640	14									
638	16									
636	18									
634	20									
632	22			seek						
630	24									
628	26			purge						
626	28									
624	30									
622	32			law found						
620	34									
618	36									
616	38									
614	40									
612	42									
610	44									
608	46									
606	48								law found	
604	50									
602	52									
600	54									
598	56									captive
596	58									
594	60									visions
592	62									
590	64									
588	66									

start ministry

THE CHRONOLOGICAL PROPHET

As a review of the biblical account of Jeremiah in chronological order, the following table outlines the basic events as they occurred. The years follow those given in the timeline. This table covers the entire book of Jeremiah and other related passages. Summaries are noted in bold text, and lists of Jeremiah's messages, which can be harder to place in chronological order, are noted with italics.

Year (BC)	Event	References
698-644	**King Manasseh Summary:** Jeremiah is a young boy growing up in Anathoth at the end of Manasseh's reign. He is perhaps as old as ten when Manasseh dies.	2 King 21:1-18 2 Chrn 33:1-20
643-642	**King Amon Summary:** Jeremiah is still a young boy growing up in Anathoth during King Amon's two-year reign.	2 King 21: 19-26 2 Chrn 33:21-25

Year (BC)	Event	References
641-610	**King Josiah Summary:** Jeremiah grows up and starts his ministry when he is perhaps twenty-five years old. He and King Josiah become good friends.	**2 King 22:1-2** **2 Chrn 34:1-2**
633	Josiah seeks God.	2 Chrn 34:3
629	Josiah starts reform.	2 Chrn 34:3-7
628	Jeremiah is commissioned in his ministry.	Jer 1:1-9
628	Jeremiah is commanded not to marry or celebrate with those who do or mourn with anyone because of the disaster that is coming.	Jer 16:1-17:18

Year (BC)	Event	References
628-610	*Jeremiah gives various prophecies and preaches during the reign of Josiah:*	
	• *Boiling Pot*	*Jer 1:11-19*
	• *God's charge against His people*	*Jer 2:1-37*
	• *Broken marriage vows*	*Jer 3:1-4:4*
	• *Disaster from the north*	*Jer 4:5-31*
	• *None righteous*	*Jer 5:1-31*
	• *Siege of Jerusalem foreseen*	*Jer 6:1-26*
	• *Jeremiah tests, but cannot refine the people*	*Jer 6:27-30*
	• *Call for righteousness. (Having the Temple won't save them)*	*Jer 7:1-29*
	• *God vs. Idols*	*Jer 10:1-16*
	• *God will expel the people from the land*	*Jer 10:17-22*
	• *Jeremiah asks for mercy in justice*	*Jer 10:23-25*
	• *Covenant is broken (given after Josiah renews covenant)*	*Jer 11:1-17*
	• *Why do the wicked prosper?*	*Jer 12:1-17*
	• *Destruction is coming (Jeremiah wishes he was never born)*	*Jer 15:1-21*
625	Drought in the land.	Jer 3:3 Jer 14:1-22
625	Jeremiah buys a jar to smash as he preaches against the false gods and child sacrifice. He is beaten and put in the stocks overnight. Then Jeremiah complains to God.	Jer 19:1-20:18 Jer 7:30-9:26

Year (BC)	Event	References
623	The Law is found. Josiah renews the covenant between God and the people and completes the purge of false religion in Judah and Israel. Finally, they celebrate the Passover.	2 King 22:3-23:28 2 Chrn 34:8-35:19
620	Jeremiah goes to the potter to see how the Creator can shape and re-shape His plans for His creation.	Jer 18:1-17
620	Priests of Anathoth try to kill Jeremiah. There is a foreshadowing of Christ's passion.	Jer 18:18-23 Jer 11:18-23 Jer 12:6
615	Jeremiah hides a linen belt, preaches about wineskins and tells the people to repent before they are taken into captivity.	Jer 13:1-27
615	Jeremiah preaches at the gates of the city about keeping the Sabbath day and not working on it.	Jer 17:19-27
610	Josiah killed in Battle against Egypt. Jeremiah composes a lament.	2 King 23:29-30 2 Chrn 35:20-27
610	**King Jehoahaz Summary:** Jehoahaz is made king. Egypt takes him captive and puts Jehoiakim on the throne as a vassal of Egypt.	**2 King 23:31-34 2 Chrn 36:1-3**

Year (BC)	Event	References
609-598	**King Jehoiakim Summary:** Jehoiakim reigns for 11 years. He is first a vassal of Egypt and then of Babylon.	**2 King 23:34-37** **2 Chrn 36:4-8**
609	Jehoiakim has Uriah, son of Shemaiah, a prophet who said the same things as Jeremiah, hunted down and killed.	Jer 26:20-23
608	Jeremiah preaches in the temple to remind the people of all that he had said over the years and give them a chance to repent and be saved. Jehoiakim bars him from going back to the temple.	Jer 26:1-19, 24
606	Nebuchadnezzar invades and takes power from Egypt. Daniel and others are taken captive to Babylon.	2 King 24:1 Dan 1:1
605	Jeremiah says that because the people have ignored God's messages through him for 23 years, Nebuchadnezzar is going to be God's servant to destroy Judah. But, after 70 years, the people will return.	Jer 25:1-14 Jer 25:15-38
605	Baruch writes out all the prophecies of Jeremiah and gets ready to read them in at the Temple since Jeremiah is barred from the Temple.	Jer 36: 1-7
605	Baruch complains to God.	Jer 45:1-5
604	Baruch reads at the Temple and Jehoiakim burns the scroll.	Jer 36:8-32

Year (BC)	Event	References
603	Jeremiah offers the Rekabite's wine.	Jer 35:1-19
600	Jeremiah preaches at the palace. He says that Jehoahaz will die in Egypt, Jehoiakim will not be honoured in death and that Jehoiachin will not be allowed to reign after his father.	Jer 22:1-30
600	Jehoiakim rebels against Nebuchadnezzar.	2 King 24:1-7
598	**King Jehoiachin Summary:** Jehoiachin surrenders to Nebuchadnezzar after 3 months and is taken captive.	**2 King 24:8-9** **2 Chrn 36:9-10**
598	Jehoiachin is taken to Babylon along with most of the articles from the temple and over 3000 captives.	2 King 24:10-17 Jer 27:19-20 Jer 52:28
597-587	**King Zedekiah Summary:** Zedekiah is made king by Nebuchadnezzar. He rebels and Jerusalem is destroyed.	**2 King 24:18-20** **2 Chrn 36:11-14** **Jer 52:1-3**
597	Nebuchadnezzar makes Zedekiah king.	Jer 37:1-2
596	Jeremiah sees two baskets of figs.	Jer 24:1-10
595	Jeremiah sends a letter to the exiles and tells them to settle down and pray for peace because God will bless them there, but it will be 70 years before they return.	Jer 29:1-32

Year (BC)	Event	References
594	Restoration of God's people foretold. The slaughter of the innocent at Christ's birth is foretold.	Jer 30:1-31:40
593	Jeremiah makes and wears a wooden yoke on his neck as a sign that captivity is coming.	Jer 27:1-18, 21-22
593	The false prophet Hananiah breaks Jeremiah's yoke.	Jer 28:1-17
591	Jerusalem is sieged.	Jer 37:5
591	Slaves are freed.	Jer 34:8-10
590	Egypt comes to aid and siege is lifted.	Jer 37:4-5
590	Slaves are retaken.	Jer 34:11
590	Jeremiah tells Zedekiah that Babylon will return and destroy the city.	Jer 34:12-22 Jer 37:3, 6-10
589	Jeremiah tries to go home to get land allocation but is arrested and put into a dungeon.	Jer 37:11-16
589	Babylon returns to besiege Jerusalem again.	2 King 25:1 Jer 39:1 Jer 52:4-5
589	Zedekiah inquires if God will deliver the city and Jeremiah tells him, "No."	Jer 21:1-14
588	Zedekiah has Jeremiah brought to the palace to see if there is a word from God.	Jer 37:17-21

Year (BC)	Event	References
588	Jeremiah buys a field.	Jer 32:1-44
588	Jeremiah prophesizes about the restoration and the coming of Jesus as our King and Priest.	Jer 33:1-26 Jer 23:1-8
588	A message about false prophets.	Jer 23:9-40
587	Jeremiah continues to preach against Jerusalem is thrown into a dry cistern.	Jer 38:1-13
587	Jeremiah tells Ebed-Melek that he will be saved when Jerusalem falls.	Jer 39:15-18
587	Zedekiah asks Jeremiah for advice.	Jer 38:14-28
587	Jeremiah has a word for Zedekiah that the city will fall but Zedekiah will survive and be honoured in death.	Jer 34:1-7
587	Jerusalem is taken.	2 King 25:2-11, 13-21 1 Chrn 36:15-20 Jer 38:28; 39:2-10 Jer 52:6-27, 29
587	**Governor Gedaliah Summary:** Jeremiah goes to live with Gedaliah and writes the book of Lamentations.	**2 King 25:12, 22-26** **Lament 1-5**
587	Jeremiah starts to be taken as a captive, but he is found and freed and goes to live under Gedaliah who was appointed governor.	Jer 39:11-14 Jer 40:1-6

Year (BC)	Event	References
587	Ishmael assassinates Gedaliah. The people flee to Egypt taking Jeremiah and Baruch with them.	Jer 40:7:43:7
587	In Egypt, Jeremiah prophesizes that Nebuchadnezzar will come there too.	Jer 43:8-44:30
582	Nebuzaradan takes another 745 Jews captive from the occupied land.	Jer 52: 30
628-586	*Other of Jeremiah's Prophecies:* • *A message to Egypt* • *A message to the Philistines* • *A message to Moab* • *A message to Ammon* • *A message to Edom* • *A message to Damascus* • *A message to Kedar and Hazor* • *A message to Elam (early in reign of Zedekiah)* • *A message to Babylon when the Jews will return home.*	*Jer. 46:1-28* *Jer. 47:1-7* *Jer. 48:1-47* *Jer. 49:1-6* *Jer. 49:7-22* *Jer. 49:23-27* *Jer 49:28-33* *Jer 49:34-39* *Jer 50:1-51:64*
565	Jehoiachin is let out of jail. He is 55 years old. He lives out his life as a guest of the king of Babylon.	2 Kings 25:27-30 Jer 52: 31-34

About the Author

Tom Birch graduated from Northwest Bible College and Seminary with a Bachelor of Theology degree. He served for a short time with Wycliffe Bible Translators and is an avid supporter of their work. His passion is to see God use the church to call the next generation back to holiness as an army for God, ministering His mercy to a hurting world. *Jeremiah: An Inspirational Guide through Troubled Times* won honourable mention in the Word Alive Press 2019 writing contest in the category of Christian non-fiction.

Contact Tom at:
trbirch@telus.net

www.ingramcontent.com/pod-product-compliance
Lightning Source LLC
Chambersburg PA
CBHW030843090426

42737CB00009B/1083